The Beauty of Balance

A Theological Inquiry into Paradox

Young Woon Ko

UNIVERSITY PRESS OF AMERICA,® INC.
Lanham • Boulder • New York • Toronto • Plymouth, UK

Copyright © 2010 by
University Press of America,® Inc.
4501 Forbes Boulevard
Suite 200
Lanham, Maryland 20706
UPA Acquisitions Department (301) 459-3366

Estover Road
Plymouth PL6 7PY
United Kingdom

All rights reserved

British Library Cataloging in Publication Information Available

Library of Congress Control Number: 2009931301
ISBN: 978-0-7618-4716-8 (paperback : alk. paper)
eISBN: 978-0-7618-4717-5

Contents

Introduction   1

1   Hegel's Dialectical Method and the System of Totality   6
2   Creativity and God in Process   22
3   Divine Paradox and Harmony in Whitehead and Jung   31
4   Bateson's Theory of Double-Binding and Meta-Context   44
5   Non-directed Order and Harmony   54
6   Wonhyo's Buddhist Thought of One Mind in the Organic Model   71
7   The Theological Significance of Paradox in the Organic Model   83

Conclusion   103

Selected Bibliography   107

Index   113

Introduction

This book examines the significance of balance between the opposites in order to understand God and the world. I will argue that the opposites—the subject and object, mind and nature, good and evil, truth and falsehood—are not separated from each other but interdependent in the relational paradigm. Each cannot exist without the other. Creative advancement is achieved by their dynamic tensions. The paradoxical relationship between the opposites is not posited in the mechanistic model in which they are recognized as separate entities and thereby antagonistic; rather they are dialectical and creative in the organic model. Based on this organic model, the relationship between God and the world is not hierarchical but interdependent.

The foundational principle of the organic model is developed not in the abstractness of concept and essence of being but in concrete phenomena understood in immediate experience as irreducible to the dualistic form of either "A" or "not A." The logical pattern of the organic model is distinguished from abstract logic or formal logic in which God and the world, good and evil, truth and falsehood are clearly divided. It is beyond the demarcation between those opposites that the correlation between contrasting poles is creatively developed in the paradoxical relation.

In this organic model, God is not described simply as a transcendent reality in a dualistic structure of God and the world. God reveals God-self in harmonious order and pattern as the ultimate principle formed in the world. In other words, God reveals God-self in the relative contexts of the opposites good and evil, true and false. Unlike Aristotle's Law of Contrast, God is both A (transcendent) and –A (immanent), which is the basic logic of the organic model. In this context, God is different from eternal reality such as Plato's Idea or the transcendent God developed in the Western tradition.

This organic model of God is found in some of the philosophical and theological arguments developed in the Western tradition. In Chapter One, I will first discuss Georg Wilhelm Hegel's (1770-1831)'s dialectical method and his philosophical and theological inquiry. I will examine Hegel's notion of synthesis in which a diversity of phenomena proceeds to unity in an absolute spirit through a dialectical logic in contrast to Aristotelian logic. In Hegel's logical system, a thing contains two opposite predicates in the interplay between its subject and object. Hegel attempts to elucidate how two opposite predicates are synthesized into a higher status in which they are not simply the conjunction of the opposite elements but that each can exist in the comprehensive idea without contradiction. Hegel's dialectic displays how the lower category is partly transformed and preserved at the level of the higher category, and the contradiction between opposite elements is dissolved in their synthesis. Hegel insists that two opposite predicates are synthesized into a higher status where they reconcile and transcend all of the contrasting categories toward the Absolute Spirit without any contradiction.

Yet, the Absolute Spirit, the ultimate stage of Hegel's dialectic, returns to Aristotle's logic, whereby all contradictions are overcome. I will critically examine Hegel's concept of the Absolute Spirit which logically keeps the Aristotelian without any paradoxical encounter between the opposite categories.

In Chapter Two, with my critical approach to both Aristotelian and Hegelian logic, I will argue that dynamic tension between the opposites is a great source of creativity in the organic model to help understand God and the world. Given this source, I will explore Whitehead's (1861-1947) philosophy of organism and discuss how he shows that the paradoxical relationship between opposites is not a negative agent to be eliminated. Rather, the positive contrast produces novelty by way of concrescence and transition. The one-many relationship in Whitehead's concept of creativity exemplifies such a paradox. Whitehead's creativity does not mean that the many proceed toward the one final reality but that the many become the one and vice-versa in a cyclical movement.

In this regard, I will discuss God in paradox and harmony, a paradigm developed by Whitehead. From Whitehead's perspective, those opposites are not antagonistic but relational and thereby become the conditions of creative transformation. In this view, God is defined by way of the paradoxical combination of opposites; God is not found in the massive movement toward goodness, but in the transformational and comprehensive whole of the contradictions. In order to explore God and creativity, I will explain Whitehead's notion of prehension, whereby God and the world paradoxically prehend each other by being affected by and affecting each other. Part of this chapter is reprinted from my review of Joseph Bracken S.J.'s *Christianity and Process Thought: Spiritual-*

ity for a Changing World (London: Templeton Foundation Press, 2006), which appears in *Process Studies* 37.2 (2008) through the courtesy of the editors and the publisher, Center for Process Studies, Claremont, California.

This process of God and the world are considered as creative ongoingness based on love. In Chapter Three, therefore, I will discuss the love of God demonstrated by Whitehead's process thought. Also, God in process is similarly shown in Jung's discussion of the conscious and the unconscious. I discuss Jung's concept of the divine in the balance between opposites, (i.e., the attunement of ego-consciousness with the depth of unconsciousness.) I recognize that this exemplification of God is made in the paradoxical combination of Jung's divine quaternity. By comparing and contrasting Whitehead with Jung, I will explain that divine paradox and harmony are the significant concepts to understanding God's love. Sections of this chapter are reprinted from my article, "Divine Paradox and Harmony in the Love of God," which appears in *The Many Facets of Love: Philosophical Explorations* (Cambridge: Cambridge Scholars Press, 2007) through the courtesy of Thomas J. Oord, the editor.

In Chapter Four, I will examine Gregory Bateson's (1904-1980) theory of "double bind" and "meta-context" in order to demonstrate the significance of a logical paradox and its contribution to the correlation between pluralist contexts. I will explain why the paradox occurs and how it can play a role in a creative agent to make a comprehensive set of opposites in the organic model. I will discuss the significance and value of the "differences" emerging from pluralist and particular contexts and how the differences can be correlated with one another and can lead to creative advances. From Bateson's perspective, the issue of religious pluralism will be explored in understanding the divine on a cross-cultural basis.

Chapter Five will examine the problem of paradox that has long been a positive and necessary element in the East Asian tradition to understand self and the world. I discuss Bertrand Russell's introduction of paradox with the problem of Aristotle's logic and explore how the issue of paradox is applied to the correlative thinking of *Yijing* formed in such opposite factors as yin and yang. Critically examining the *Yijing* theory and language in terms of paradoxical combination and harmony, I will introduce Ilbu Kim's (1828-1889) *Jeongyeokdo* and Jaewoo Choi's (1824-1864) Donghak movement as a new paradigm for the theme of paradox and demonstrate how they contribute to setting a theory of divine order and harmony by breaking the barrier between the opposites. Sections of this chapter is reprinted from my article "The Issue of Paradox and Creativity of *Jeongyeok* in the Language of *Yijing*," which appears in *Studies on Religions of Korea* (Seoul: The Association of Korean Native Religions, 2006) through the courtesy of Sang Yil Kim, the editor.

Ilbu Kim's and Jaewoo Choi's correlative thoughts are in sequence with Wonhyo's (617-86), *Hwajaeing* thoughts developed in the Korean Buddhist tradition. Wonhyo's *Hwajaeing*, or "Harmonization of All Disputes," takes the epistemological shift to harmony and reconciliation beyond binary opposites and conflicts. By identifying the disintegration of the world with that of the mind, Wonhyo examines the possibility of the integration of the world through that of the mind. Through Wonhyo's thoughts on the One Mind and *Hwajaeing* methods, in Chapter Six, I will argue that mind is not simply the subjective mind but the mind organically connected with other minds. The true reality, or the divine, resides in the non-discriminatory character of the One Mind. The One Mind as the source of all life indicates the indivisible state of mind, which is identified with the Buddha Mind based on great compassion and emancipation.

In Chapter Seven I will discuss the theological significance of paradox in the organic model. I will explore how the complex of divine reality entails the dialogue of differences in a constructive way: interreligious dialogue and religion-nature dialogue. In particular, I will discuss the dialogue between Christianity and nature and the dialogue between Christianity and other world religions. Interreligious dialogue and environmental ethics are the subjects that challenge the Christian tradition, which has focused on individual salvation without considering the organic relation to natural environments and to other religious contexts. In the midst of these dialogues, some contrasting elements give rise, and yet they should not be regarded as pathological but creative sources to construct a bigger horizon of theological perspectives. I will bring Sallie McFague into my discussion of the organic model of Christianity and natural environments. Edward Farley's symbolism and Peter Schineller's four positions of Christology will also be discussed to bring insight into religious pluralism.

In the conclusion, I summarize my theological inquiry into paradox and argue the beauty of balance in the encounter between opposites. The beauty of balance does not eliminate "ambiguities" or paradoxes arising in their dynamic tensions. I maintain that the ambiguities and paradoxes are the aesthetic sources of creativity and God. The ambiguities as aesthetic sources are not negative objects but creative agents to be transformed into the beauty of balance. Given this aesthetic mode of balance between contrasts, I present the theological significance of the organic model for overcoming religious conflicts and ecological problems that our contemporary world faces.

While there is plenty of literature on interreligious dialogue and ecological theology, a dearth exists of theological approaches to those themes in the affirmation of paradox. In particular, paradox has been regarded as fallible or pathological in the history of Western thought; it has been something negative to be eliminated. On the contrary, I will bring the theme of paradox into my discussion to connect the West with the East and explore how it can be a positive source to understanding God and the world in the organic model, which can be a key to the understanding of the common good.

Chapter One

Hegel's Dialectical Method and the System of Totality

Hegel's view of reality is developed in the dynamical movement which proceeds to absolute spirit. According to Hegel, when the spirit as the immediate self is externalized in the mediation of other objects, it appears as nature, and then when the spirit returns to and knows itself as the universal self, it becomes the absolute sprit. Hegel explains the process of three stages toward absolute spirit as "being-in-itself (*An-sich-Sein*)," "being for-itself (*Fur-sich-Sein*)," "being in-and-for-itself (*An-und-fur-sich-Sein*)" and expresses the spirits corresponding to those three stages as subjective spirit, objective spirit, and absolute spirit.[1]

> The developmental process of Hegel's absolute spirit is essentially based on the mediation of the logical idea through which spirit does not fall into its solipsism but relates itself to nature: First, nature is the mediating member. Nature, that immediate totality, unfolds itself into two extremes, the logical idea and spirit. But spirit is spirit only insofar as it is mediated by nature. Secondly, spirit—known by us as individual and active—is the middle, and nature and the logical idea are the extremes. For it is spirit which recognizes the idea in nature and raises nature to its essence. Thirdly, the logical idea is itself the middle. It is the absolute substance of both spirit and nature, that which is universal and all-penetrating.[2]

Nature, spirit, and the logical idea produce different features of spirit in mediating one another. Nature as middle factor brings "naturalism" or objective spirit, while the spiritual mediation causes "subjective idealism" or subjective spirit. Yet Hegel bases his philosophical system upon the mediation of the logical idea as the universal principle or substance to construct "absolute idealism" or absolute spirit, wherein spirit and nature are extended through the concrete representation of absolute reason. Peter Hodgson states the following about the modes of spirit by the mediating principle in Hegel's system:

If nature were to become the universal principle, then spirit would be mediated with its particular (now merely logical) qualities by means of nature itself, and the resulting system would be naturalism. If finite spirit were to become the universal principle, then nature would be mediated with its particular (logical) qualities by means of spirit itself, which would be an instance of subjective idealism. . . . The alternative requires the transcendence of the logical idea as the universal principle rather than its immanence in nature and finite spirit as their particular logical qualities; this transcendence of the idea yields Hegel's absolute or objective idealism.[3]

Hegel assumes that spirit and nature are not reduced to each other in the universal principle of the logical idea. In the correlation of spirit and nature, spirit neither falls into individual finite spirit nor into the particular quality of nature. Nature is neither reduced to subjective idealism nor to naturalism. As Hodgson says, "nature is the pre-self of spirit, and spirit is the telos of nature."[4] The two extremes reveal their own stances in their interaction through dialectical processes in the mediation of the logical ideas as the universal principle. Spirit and nature accomplish their self-manifestation in each other. On the other hand, the natural mediation reduces individual spirit to naturalism while the spiritual mediation dilutes nature into subjectivism.[5]

Spirit is therefore not only the substance but also the movement and process in relation to nature. This exists in the human being but should not be identified with the human spirit. For it is the absolute and essential reality in the world whose process is the movement of spirit. In this process, spirit has its objective form and reaches complete self-recognition. Spirit characterizes its generation and development in the process of thought.[6]

The self-manifestation of spirit is the embodiment of the truth in the process that contains all occasions in the logical reasoning for reaching the ultimate totality. Hegel asserts that, in logical reasoning, the object of reasoning is formed in the process of reasoning. In this structure, history is the expression and process of reasoning and of the development of the spirit itself. The phenomenon of history is the concrete expression of the world spirit (i. e., absolute spirit), dialectically constituted in the process of reasoning. "What is rational, is actual and what is actual, is rational." "What is ultimate real is the self-knowing spirit."[7] According to Hegel, rationality is in actuality, and actuality is in rationality, thereby realizing the spirit of self-manifestation. Hegel develops the process of reasoning and rationality from the concept of being:

The doctrine of the Concept subdivides into: (1) the doctrine of the subjective or formal Concept, (2) that of objectivity or of the Concept as determined to immediacy, (3) that of the Idea, or of the Subject-Object, the unity of the Concept and of objectivity, the absolute truth.[8]

In other words, the Concept is the Concept always interlinked to the reality, whereby the dialectical interaction of the subject and the object constitutes a coherent whole in which the Concept is one with the absolute truth. In relationship with the object, the subjective or formal Concept does not remain in itself but meets the opposite to its original predicate and transforms the Concept itself in relation to the opposite. In this sense Hegel's logic does not follow Aristotle's Law of Contradiction in which a subject cannot have the predicates of both A and -A.[9] In Hegel's logical system, a thing contains two opposite predicates in the interplay of its subject and object. Hegel insists that two opposite predicates are synthesized in a higher status where they are not simply the conjunction of the opposite elements but exist in the comprehensive idea without contradiction. In this development, the fusion of thought and being is accomplished in the concept through which being reflects the rational structure of thought. Being is the enduring process in which the principle of rationality is realized in actuality.

The combination of the opposites and the unity of thought and being are developed in the dialectical structure underlying Hegel's philosophical system. Hegel's dialectics display how the lower category is partly transformed and preserved at the level of higher category at the same time as the contradiction of opposite elements are dissolved in their synthetic totality.[10] In this fashion two opposite categories can be paradoxically true about one subject. In this situation we require the third category whenever employing the first and second category, so that the contradiction is sublated in the third term (*aufheben*). This third term, however, is not a simple addition of the two opposites but includes their descriptions in which thesis and antithesis are dynamically moved in the synthesis of the subject and the object.[11] That is to say, the dialectical movement arises in the opposition and inconsistency caused by the discordance of the Concept with reality, thereby requiring the process of the synthesis and reconciling both extreme opposites.

In this movement, we cannot eliminate the contradiction until reaching the ending point of the ladder made up of categories. At this point Hegel's dialectics start in the simplest idea or the Concept of spirit and end with the idea that confirms itself in the subject-object unity, the category that Hegel regards as the highest idea realizing the absolute truth.

For Hegel, the absolute truth is the dynamic reality formed in unceasing dialectical process rather than static and fixed reality. Through the dialectical process the abstractness of the Concept proceeds to the concreteness in which the contradictory phenomena of the Concept are presented to the Concept itself and reconcile themselves by manifesting one into the other.

> The Concept as such contains the moment of universality, as free equality with itself in its determinacy; it contains the moment of particularity, or of

Hegel's Dialectical Method and the System of Totality 9

the determinacy in which the Universal remains serenely equal to itself; and it contains the moment of singularity, as the inward reflection of the determinacies of universality and particularity. This singular negative unity with itself is what is in and for itself determined, and at the same time identical with itself or universal.[12]

The Concept includes both the moments of universality and particularity in the Concept itself. The universality reveals itself not in the moment separated from the particularity but in its determinacy by way of which universality embodies and realizes itself in particularity. Particularity overcomes the self-inconsistency in its realization of universality, which follows the process of negation.

According to Hegel, negation has the productive and creative characteristics to reach the higher level of unity. For the determinacy of a self, it concretely experiences the particularity of itself in relation to other selves and does not remain in the single particularity per se but proceeds to the higher realm of unity through the process of negation in a series of dialectical moments. In this situation the particularity, negation, and the universality cannot be understood as separated occasions but as the process connected with one another toward the totality of the absolute truth in Hegel's philosophical system.

THE LINEAR OF THE CIRCULAR IN HEGEL

Above all, Hegel emphasizes the unity of the subject and the object in understanding the spirit or the mind. He drives the structure of all existences into the dialectical and relational process in which the subject and object are conceived not of static substances but of dynamic movement.

In this dialectical process Hegel's system shows a linear pattern proceeding toward the absolute spirit. The concept of religion is extended in its encounter with the reality of religious experiences, and the reestablished concept manifests the absolute spirit. The absolute idea in Hegel is the production of various mediations in dialectical ways rather than an atomic event. It requires the process of the correlation of the opposites, thereby overcoming the naturalism and subjective idealism of the finite spirit. Thus, the absolute spirit results from the third term emerging after the mediation conforming to "lived experience."[13]

In Hegel's system, of course, a circular movement is also emphasized in a linear pattern. For the subject and the object are synthesized in the whole process of negations, whereby they are circularly incorporated in the absolute spirit. In this regard Hodgson states:

> The movement of Hegel's thought is both circular and linear; it is, in other words, that of a helix of helical spiral. He stands between the Greek and

Romantic fascination with the circle and the biblical view of salvation-history as a linear, teleological process. The two perspectives are reconciled in and transfigured by the Christian doctrine of the Trinity; the triune God is eternally self-complete, yet continually enriches or 'spiritualizes' himself in the world-historical process.[14]

In other words, Hegel's system can be said to *be the linear of the circular* by fusing the circular movement with Christian teleological process, which causes the spiral movement. God and world history are circulated in the triune God at the stage of the absolute spirit but follow a linear pattern to reach the ultimate totality through the negation of negations. In other words, the circular movement appears in the absolute spirit toward which the linear structure is formed through the process of mediation, thereby attempting to avoid the reductive way of naturalism and subjective ideality and attaining the fullness and enrichment of the spirit.

In his recognition of temporality, Hegel does not regard the past, the present, and the future as separated moments. History is the expression of the development of the spirit itself. The phenomena of history are the concrete expressions of the world spirit. The past, the present, and the future are developed in the necessary law of the reason in a dialectical process. On the other hand, Hegel's system requires historical development toward synthesis in order to reveal the final absolute spirit. The absolute spirit is developed through the phases of finitude as its prior step for the total synthesis of the spirit in-and-for itself toward which all determinate experiences are cumulatively penetrated in the process of historical development.

From this point of view, Hegel shows cumulative processes in his system of totality. Hegel's dialectical scheme manifests the process of the penetration whose degree is cumulatively intensified in the dialectical process of synthesis, whereby the spirit reconciles itself with nature and returns to its essence in the totality.

THE SIGNIFICANCE OF BUDDHIST-CHRISTIAN DIALOGUE IN HEGEL'S PHILOSOPHY OF RELIGION

Hegel brings the synthetic system of Concept and reality to the discussion of the determinate and consummate religions with the finite and infinite dialectical relation. He maintains that determinateness is the necessary process for synthesis or the totality of the absolute spirit. Religious traditions and experiences are explicated through the determinate forms of religion in which the finite reflects itself and proceeds to the infinite.

In order to realize the absolute truth and totality, the dialectical activity expands one's thought within the Concept into the realities, which bring us to a diversity of cultural and religious traditions and views. The Concept should link itself to various religious experiences with its determinateness *"in and for itself."* As Hodgson says, "the Concept [for Hegel] has the provision of a preliminary description of religion, including a derivation of its concept from its appearance in the various forms of religion."[15] The Concept of religion includes a diversity of religious forms in its essential feature which is not constrained in Concept itself. The Concept shows itself in its determinateness by way of which it turns into the opposite and forms itself in reality. Hegel says,

> There can be but one method in all science, in all knowledge. Method is just the self-explicating concept—nothing else—and the concept is one only. Here, too, therefore, the first moment is, as always, the concept. The second moment is the determinateness of the concept, the concept in its determinate forms. These forms are necessarily involved in the concept itself.[16]

The Concept without its determinateness is incomplete and does not connect itself with the activity of existence in which the Concept is displayed. Determinateness is the activity of the Concept in the finite through which the activity of negation in the process of which the opposite relationship between the finite and the infinite urges the dialectical movement.

> The determinate concept of religion, then is religion in its finitude, finite religion, something one-sided constituted in opposition to other religions as one particular type set against another. For that reason we consider in the third place the concept as it comes forth to itself out of its determinateness, out of its finitude, as it reestablishes itself out of its own finitude, its own confinement. This reestablished concept is the infinite, true concept, the absolute idea or the true religion.[17]

In its particularity, the determinateness of religion shows the finitude of one-sided constitution, thereby making distinctions from other religious contexts. For instance, Buddhist samsara and nirvana reflect the Buddhist tradition based on the cyclical experience of the secular and the sacred. This manifests the unique characteristic that distinguishes Buddhism from other religious traditions such as Judaism or Islam. Each religion has its own uniqueness that can create a contradictory relationship with other religions. These finite characteristics of determinate religions should thus reestablish themselves toward absolute and infinite ideas from which the true religion emerges. Hegel states that

> in determinate religion as such, in finite religion, we have before us only subordinate determinations of spirit or of religion we do not yet have the religion

of absolute truth. But the progression [of finite religion] is a condition for the arrival of religion at its absolute truth, for spirit's coming to be for spirit, for the relationship of spirit to spirit, a condition for the attainment by spirit itself of its truly infinite determinateness.[18]

The determinate religion is not yet the stage in which the absolute spirit is manifested, wherein the spirit knows itself. Yet the determinateness of spirit in finite religions is the necessary condition to reach the phase of the true infinite. The absolute spirit is realized in the process produced by finding the inconsistency of the finite religions and thus in the continuous movement toward the infinite. The infinite is the term not antithetical to the finite but encompassing it and thereby necessarily requires the finite and determinate moments in and for the spirit.

Hegel regards Buddhism as a determinate religion, the spirit of which is not yet free and actual.[19] Hegel's description of Buddhism appears differently in his lectures on the philosophy of religion. While Hegel defines Buddhism as "the Religion of Being-Within-Self" in his 1824 lectures, he pays more attention to the Buddhist notion of emptiness or nirvana in his 1827 lectures. Hegel also describes Buddhism as "the Religion of Annihilation" in his 1831 Lectures.[20] Yet, throughout all those lectures, the Buddhist spirit is not yet free from nature. Hegel develops his interpretation of Buddhism by focusing on "negation" (i.e., annihilation).

> One has to make nothingness of oneself. Within one's being one has to behave in this negative way, to resist not what is external but only oneself. The state that is represented as a human being's goal, this state of unity and purity, the Buddhists call nirvana. . . . When one is no longer subjected to the burdens of stress, old age, sickness, and death, nirvana has been attained; one is then identical with God is regarded as God himself, has become Buddha.[21]

Nirvana is achieved in the activity of negation accomplished within our mind. From Hegel's perspective, Buddhist negation is the activity for eliminating one's own stress and the agony existing in one's internal mind and self. Buddhist dialectical relation is carried out by continuously negating any grasping in one's mind, not by mediating the contradiction between the internal subject and external object. In this sense, for Hegel, Buddhist ultimate reality is also understood only as the immanent being in the mind. There is no transcendent aspect of God in the notion of nirvana.

At this point Hegel understands Buddhist ultimate reality in the pantheistic view. The absolute and the world are one substance. "[In Buddhism] we find the form of substantiality in which the absolute is a being-within-self, the one substance."²² The sacred and the secular are one substance in which the ultimate exists within one's self, i.e., the Buddha-mind.

Hegel regards the Buddhist ultimate reality as the indeterminate being with whom the self is unified by negating everything particular.²³ Buddhist God is not represented and mediated by something particular. From this perspective, Buddhist spirit is immersed in the immediate subjectivity. "What is spiritual is still in immediate, sensible existence, and this subjectivity is still an immediate subjectivity."²⁴ From Hegel's perspective, the spirit in Buddhism does not make self-recognition in immediate relation to and one substance with nature. It does not yet make the synthetic system of the spiritual immediacy and mediation in which one makes self-manifestation and enters the higher realm of the spirit by the mediation of the third moment.

Hegel's system of totality, above all, accentuates the freedom of spirit in the dialectical process of spirit and nature without reducing the importance of either. In this context, Hegel understands Buddhism as the phase in which the spirit does not mediate itself with its opposite and therefore does not draw the absolute spirit that brings freedom beyond all contrasting relations

Hegel's view of Buddhism is somewhat limited by his driving Buddhist notions into a uniform context. As Hodgson mentions, "he [Hegel] developed a vast knowledge of world religions, flawed only by the inadequate scientific basis for the study of religions that prevailed in his time."²⁵ Hegel's Buddhist understanding is based on some select translated materials, not on the wide array of Buddhist sutras and treatises and schools. Another problematic point is that Hegel frames Buddhism into the structure of his philosophical system. In this view, it is easy to lose some pivotal points about Buddhism. For instance, Buddhism denies any view that the ultimate reality and the self are understood as one substance, that their fundamental structure is relational. The Buddhist tradition emphasizes that nirvana and the individual self is the one and the many without one reducing the other.

For the consummate religion, Hegel is deeply concerned with the self-manifestation found in the realization of the spirit (both divine and human) in the historical process. As a result, the philosophical truth developed in his thought is the penetration between God and the human being, whereby God is revealed through human history. Hegel argues that Christianity is the consummate or revelatory religion, as the synthesis of natural religion and artistic religion (as found in Greece). According to Hegel, Christianity is based on "the idea of God in and for itself" through the immanent trinity and supplements the finite moments of other religions in the developmental process of "creation, fall, incarnation, and redemption."²⁶ The real and historical unification of God and the human being is accomplished in God's incarnation.

For Hegel, the three phases of the reality of God—essential being, represented self-existence, and self-knowledge—function in the process of realizing the agreement between the divine and the human. The first phase is pure, abstract being; the second is the stage when abstract spirit emerges as existence through the creation of the world. The world as "objectively existent spirit" is characterized by being "the Son" (i.e., the being recognizing itself as the essential being) and the estrangement and abandonment (evil). The third phase occurs when the spirit enters self-consciousness.[27]

Hegel's stages of God's reality bring the contact of the consummate religion and philosophical truth wherein absolute spirit appears, and God is self-conscious in human beings. The first stage is God as the essential or primordial being. The second stage is God in relation to others out of God's primordial and abstract vision. God returns to Godself in human beings in the consequent nature. In other words, God is conscious of God-self in the religious life where the human being also becomes aware of God. This is the third stage in which God and the human being are reconciled in reality. This nature of God reveals the pan-en-theistic view of God, wherein divine immanence and transcendence are articulated simultaneously.

According to Hegel, Christianity describes this process through creation and redemption. He argues that creation necessarily includes estrangement by transference to the individual being. Hegel accentuates the necessary movement from the Fall to self-consciousness in history. Hegel agrees with the traditional theology that regards the Fall as evil in that human history accompanies the disunion and estrangement. However, this process of the Fall is also the necessary stage which causes the dialectical moment and the reconciliation between God and the human being.[28]

Through the significance of Christ-event, the agreement of God and the human being in Jesus is manifested historically. The God-human agreement through God's incarnation is realized in Jesus as a historical individual. Because history is the actual development of reality, this event has a great significance to God. In other words, God is transferred from abstract thought to historical and concrete individuality, and in this process, achieves the consummate reality and the freedom of the spirit in history. In Hegel's view, Jesus' resurrection is the emergence of the absolute spirit in God's historical realization as the moment of reconciliation.[29]

Therefore philosophy and Christianity converge with each other by focusing on synthesis and reconciliation in an attempt to overcome opposition, inconsistency, and alienation. The absolute spirit is accomplished in the historical process of the world by concretizing the spirit. By doing so, the absolute spirit offers the meaning of spirit to each individual element constituting the world and history, embodies the spirit itself in the human form and image, and reconciles itself with the world in the infusion of time and eternity.

Hegelian dialectics can offer the constructive method for the encounter of Christianity with Buddhism. Since the Hegelian methodology attempts to encompass all antithetical positions and find the absolute spirit through God's actuality in the concrete phenomena of world, it draws the interreligious dialogue that reconciles some contrasting religious doctrines and experiences.

However, Hegel's understanding of Buddhism shows some limitations for Christian-Buddhist dialogue. Even though Hegel revealed the significant knowledge of Buddhism unlike other 19th-century philosophers and theologians, he did not have the opportunity to see Buddhist texts as much as Christian texts.[30] Yet Hegel makes detailed analyses of given materials and shows his deep concern with the relation between the self and nature in Buddhism. According to Walter Jaeschke,

> Hegel's efforts to achieve a critical understanding of the history of religion are at the service of his theory of absolute spirit and, more specifically, the historical dimension of spirit. To this extent the history of religion forms an indispensable moment in Hegel's conception of his system, along with other partial histories of absolute and objective spirit—in the histories of art, of philosophy, and world-history.[31]

Hegel's criticism of Buddhism is understood with reference to his development of absolute spirit. Hegel develops his understanding of the history of religion in his purpose on the actualization of the objective spirit in the dialectical process through which the world religions are examined in terms of the history of spirit and of pre-stages for the consummate religion. Hegel treats Buddhism at the level of a subsidiary role to approach the infinite spirit based on Christianity.

Hegel, of course, shows his expanding knowledge of Buddhism in a series of his lectures. According to Hodgson,

> This is Buddhism, the religion of 'being-within-self' or 'self-containment,'. . . . Unfortunately, Hegel's sources and his knowledge of Buddhism were not adequate to the importance assigned to this religion—an importance assigned almost intuitively, perhaps, through a recognition of the speculative significance of the concept of nirvana, which is, however, only briefly discussed in 1824. . . . Buddhism is now a distinct stage, as warranted by its religio-historical significance as an axial religion, and Hegel in 1827 directs more attentions to its fundamental conception of ultimate reality as "nothing" or nirvana. To say that God is nothing does not mean that God is not but rather that God is nothing determinate, the negation of everything particular, the unitary universal, "the empty": thereby an important dimension of the truth about God is expressed. This is the truth grasped by Oriental pantheism in contrast to the Western preoccupation with individuality. . . . The distinctive leitmotif of the 1831 lectures

is the role played by religion in the history of the consciousness of freedom the emergence of freedom out of nature, first through the cleavage of consciousness (the Oriental religions), . . .[32]

Hegel's initial understanding of Buddhism is the idea of "being-within-self," wherein the self is regarded as being reduced to nature. The self is understood in no difference from nature. Hegel then brings out the concrete notion of nirvana based on nothingness or emptiness, which is not reduced to any particular structure. Nirvana does not manifest any sense of individuality. It draws the negation of any quality in nature but does not posit the particular individuality. In this context, Hodgson describes Hegel's view of Buddhism as "the religion of annihilation," an expression from Hegel's lectures of 1831. But as Hodgson contends, this Buddhist perspective is based on pantheism in terms of a theological aspect. Emptiness means rather the fullness wherein no separate beings exist, so that the truth is realized in this actual world through the process of self-annihilation. In this sense, we cannot posit any transcendent personal reality differentiated from the world, thereby leading to pantheistic view.

One of the difficulties in easily understanding Buddhism in theological terms is that Buddhism is based on a different paradigm from Christianity. This difficulty may be in the disparity between basic assumptions of the two religious traditions. The discussions of theism, pantheism, or pan-en-theism may be the discussions operated in terms of the Christian tradition. The terms such as "theistic," "pantheistic," "pan-en-theistic," can be inadequate to describe the essential nature of Buddhahood. This problem can arise if we discuss God's trinity with Buddhist terms such as *tathagata*, *gharba*, *gotra*.[33] In this regard Frank Reynolds maintains the following:

> A closely related positive aspect of Hegel's treatment of Buddhism has to do with the underlying problematic which he utilizes to structure his discussion— namely the question of how Buddhism addresses and grapples with the issues with a notion of human freedom that was radically restricted by his own ontology; and as a result he was prevented from taking seriously the way in which the relevant issues arise and are dealt with in the Buddhist context.[34]

Reynolds's remark indicates that Hegel's notion of freedom in absolute reason and spirit is different from the Buddhist notion of freedom. From Hegel's perspective, Buddhism does not articulate any sense of human freedom due to its emphasis of interdependence. From the Buddhist perspective, however, human freedom is shaped not in the totality of dialectical relationship but in the emptiness realized at every moment. In the Hegelian view, such Buddhist opinion is incomplete due to its failure to realize the freedom of the human spirit liberated from any finite spirit that does not yet combine all the opposite phenomena and thus does not actualize the synthetic moment. In Buddhism, however, the human freedom is also in the One Mind that embraces all others in the interdependent relation reached through the negation of any conceptual or thinking system that can obstruct freedom. One total mind does not require the mediation of dialectical process but is practiced at every moment. In this context, these two different religious traditions need to be examined by respecting the differences of each and recognizing them as equals.

Yet, Hegel's whole idea shows the importance of the Christian-Buddhist dialogue. Hegel's system is, above all, enhanced in our experience as well as reason, thereby dialectically accommodating novelty arising in our encounter with others. As Hodgson writes,

> Hegel clearly recognizes that empirically and historically based experience presents an endlessly novel and to some degree unexpected temporal flow, which can never be predicted a priori. Without the impingement of this positive content, there would be no reality for us. His reference to the embodiment of particular logical categories in particular phases of nature and concrete spirit remain irregular and inconsistent, and he rarely attempts precise correlations. But on the other hand, Hegel's conviction that thought and sense have a single source, and that form and content are inseparable.[35]

Unlike Aristotle's law of contradiction and excluded middle in which a proposition should be either true or false, Hegel's logic uses contradictory propositions as the agents for producing the novelty through the process of affirmation-negation. It combines opposite sides into one creative whole. It combines the transcendental and the immanent being. The idea of Hegelian synthesis cannot be established without the experience of the reality representing the paradoxical oneness of the one and the many. It shows thus illogical and inconsistent aspects in the dialectical process in contrast with Aristotle's logic, but all paradoxical situations are ultimately dissolved and developed into the novel synthesis of the reason and experience, the thought and being.

In this regard, Yu-Hui Chen emphasizes this significance in the interplay of Hegel and Buddhism in his book *Absolutes Nichts und rhythmisches Sein*.

> For Hegel, a being can be also described as nothingness; nothingness is regarded not only as the contradictory opposite to being, but also, to a certain extent, as the definition of being. . . . Hegel's conception reminds us of "non-duality" in Zen-Buddhism. . . . From the view of Zen-master, the ultimate being is grasped not through the structure of either/or, wherein the positive is driven into the negative in a strict way. The structure of being breaks down through them [affirmation and negation] and penetrates the two opposite for being itself.[36]

Although Chen specifically delimits his subject in Zen tradition, the nonduality and nothingness of Zen Buddhism are commonly shown in most Buddhist traditions (such as Huayen and T'iendai). Hegel do not understand reality in the system of "either/or." He observes reality in nothingness, which is not reduced into a fixed certainty but continuously accomplishes self-transformation without any simple location in encountering with others.

This character of Hegelian ideas provides a significant method for the encounter of Christianity with Buddhism. Since their ideas attempt to encompass the differences of each other in the relational paradigm, Christianity and Buddhism can be creatively transformed by enriching the experiences of each other. Their ideas do not stay simply in the distinct aspects of the religions but instead instigate wider perspectives, thereby practicing self-transformation and fructifying the expansive horizon. That philosophical system does not simply combine only the mutual common items but rather works in a dialectical way to enrich the life experiences of different religions.

For Hegel, because all concepts and ideas are tested in light of actual and concrete experiences, the *a-posteriori* contents are not led by *a-priori* form. Our idea and concept are endlessly transformed by new contents. In this respect the Hegelian system is open to the actuality of the world and to various religious experiences.

Hegel's ideas contribute to the interreligious dialogue with mutual supplementation. For the two philosophical systems, the ultimate reality is not a static entity. It is created by reconciling all opposite contexts and thus producing a new transformation. Hegel's idea of Absolute Spirit does not reduce some antithetical situations into the alternative way of true or false but encompass them to achieve creative synthesis. In this regard the Christian-Buddhist dialogue is an attempt to enrich one's own tradition by learning other religious traditions and transforming and growing and creating new life in dynamic, processing, and dialectical ways. Hodgson describes the significance of the Christian-Buddhist dialogue:

> The tendency of all religion is to universalize their cultural particularities rather than their disclosures of truth. Thus Christianity has tended to absolutize its scriptures, its institutional forms, its dogmatic claims about God, Christ, sin, and salvation, rather than what is truly distinctive about Christian ecclesiastical existence, which is its radical gratuity, its intrinsic nonprovinciality.... The encounter of the religious also provides a way of drawing out and reinforcing the capacities for self-transcendence and truth that are present in the great religious traditions. The dialogue between Buddhism and Christianity has gone farthest in this regard, with Buddhism providing insight into the Christian understanding of grace as a radical detachment or letting-go, and Christianity providing deepened insight into the Buddhist understanding of selfhood and freedom.[37]

The real task for interreligious dialogue is found not in religious syncretism or the relativity of the gospel but rather in the question of whether the different religious expressions of other religions can reconcile each other in the creative synthesis. The encounter of Christianity with Buddhism is not compromising but creative. For instance, Buddhism can learn the notion of freedom from Hegelian absolute spirit. As David Griffin indicates, Buddhist doctrines lack self-autonomous implications, and every event lacks any power of self-determination for its own sake.[38] Because Buddhist thoughts emphasize the interdependence and co-origination of all occasions throughout the whole systems, we can have difficulty observing self-determination free from other events in the Buddhist tradition. Buddhism can develop the idea of freedom from the absolute spirit that has self-autonomous moments in connection with others.

On the other hand, the Hegelian system can learn overcoming all forms of verbalization, speculative thinking, and conceptualization from the Buddhist tradition. Even if Hegel does not intend a sheer systemic and speculative process, his whole thought is often understood as emphasizing reason over feeling and driving all existential relation to the system of totality. Kierkegaard's and Troeltsch's criticisms of the Hegelian system illustrate that problem.[39] At this point Hegelian totality can learn the spirit of detachment beyond any speculative system from Buddhist ideas.

Hegel's dialectical way highlights practicing the endless self-transformation beyond their distinctions. Using such a method promotes interreligious dialogue. Their methodologies always open the door to a new phenomenon of opposite categories and thus enhance the encounter of different religions and thoughts because their philosophical systems are continuously constructed through others. Differences in the two traditions should be reflected upon in light of the other, and in doing so, highlight their uniqueness in relationship and transform their own tradition in dialogue. In this sense the dialogue between Christianity and Buddhism is formed by admitting and respecting each other's identities and lives. In this encounter, each religious tradition can learn about the other and thereby make one's own experience more powerful.

NOTES

1. G. W. F. Hegel, *Phenomenology of Spirit*, trans. A. V. Miller (Oxford: Oxford University Press, 1977), 17-8; *G. W. F. Hegel Theologian of the Spirit,* ed. Peter C. Hodgson (Minneapolis: Fortress Press, 1997), 8.

2. Quoted from Peter Hodgson, "Georg Wilhelm Friedrich Hegel" in *Nineteenth Century Religious Thought in the West*, ed. Ninian Smart vol. 1 (Cambridge: Cambridge University Press, 1985), 82.

3. Ibid., 83.
4. Ibid.
5. Ibid. Hodgson describes Hegel's system of U (the universal principle, the logical idea), P (the particular quality, nature), and I (the individual subject, spirit) as follows: "1. The natural mediation: U-P-I. The logical idea is the principle of nature; spirit is embodied in nature as pre-self or other-than-self; therefore spirit is founded not in itself but in the logical idea, and the logical idea is the principle of spirit. 2. The spiritual mediation: U-I-P. The logical idea is the principle of spirit; nature has its telos in spirit; therefore nature is raised to its essence in the logical idea, and the logical idea is the principle of nature. The logical mediation: P-U-I. Nature has its principle in the logical idea; spirit has its principle in the logical idea; therefore nature and spirit are co-extensive in the sense that nature is the principle of spirit, and spirit is the telos of nature."
6. Hegel, *Theological of the Spirit,* ed. Hodgson, 8-11.
7. T. M. Knox, "Translator's Preface," in Hegel, *Aesthetics: Lecture on Fine Art*, trans. T. M. Knox, vol. 1 (Oxford: Clarendon Press, 1999), ix.
8. Hegel, *The Encyclopaedia Logic :Part I of the Encyclopaedia of Philosophical Sciences with Zusatze*, trans. T.F. Geraets, W.A. Suchting, H.S. Harris (Cambridge: Hackett Publishing Company, Inc), 238.
9. Aristotle's logic represents Law of Identity (A is A), Law of Contradiction (A cannot be both A and not A), and Law of Excluded Middle (A must be either A or not A). These logical systems are based on conceptual and abstract thinking in quest for the essence of the world so that they thereby regard any dynamic change and contradictories as a logical fallacy. See *Aristotle's Categories and Propositions*, translated with commentaries and glossary by Hippocrates G. Apostle (Grinnell, Iowa: The Peripatetic Press, 1980), 30-48.
10. Stephen Houlgate, *Freedom, Truth and History: An Introduction to Hegel's Philosophy* (London: Routledge, 1991), 61-2.
11. Raymond Keith Williamson, *Introduction to Hegel's Philosophy of Religion* (Albany, NY: SUNY, 1984), 114--5.
12. Hegel, *The Encyclopaedia Logic :Part I of the Encyclopaedia of Philosophical Sciences with Zusatze*, 232.
13. Hodgson, "Georg Wilhelm Friedrich Hegel" in *Nineteenth Century Religious Thought in the West*, 83.
14. Ibid., 84.
15. Hegel, *Lectures on the Philosophy of Religion, One-Volume Edition The Lectures of 1827*, ed. Peter C. Hodgson (Berkeley, CA: University of California Press, 1988), 16.
16. Ibid., 101.
17. Ibid., 102.
18. Ibid., 204.
19. Ibid., 207.
20. Ibid., 499.
21. Ibid., 255.
22. Ibid., 252.

23. Ibid., 256.
24. Ibid., 267.
25. Hodgson, "G. W. F. Hegel" in *Nineteenth Century Religious Thought* in the West, 94.
26. Ibid., 102.
27. Hegel, *Lectures on the Philosophy of Religion*, 417-89.
28. Hegel, *Lectures on the Philosophy of Religion*, 446-57.
29. Ibid., 452-70.
30. Walter Jaeschke, "Between Myth and History: On Hegel's Study of The History of Religion," in *AAR Nineteenth Century Theology Group 1992*, 69. That is to say, he did not have sufficient materials for understanding Buddhism in a complexity and diversity of various schools and traditions such as Hinayana and Mahayana (Yogakara, Pure Land, Madhyamika, Tendai, Zen, Hua-yen, etc.).
31. Ibid., 68.
32. Hodgson, "Logic, History, and Alternative Paradigms in Hegel's Interpretation of the Religions," in *AAR Nineteenth Century Theology Group 1992*, 9, 11, 13.
33. These are the Sanskrit words corresponding to the idea of Buddha nature in the case of Buddha-nature-in-all-beings in *Ratnagotravibhaga*, the theory of Buddha's Matrix. Buddha nature is the compound predicate combining some of the three words-*dhatu* (nature), *garba* (matrix), *tathagata* (Thus-come or Absolute Reality). In these words, *dhatu* means the element or ingredient with which one can become buddha, *garbha* means the state in which Buddha is in the womb as an embryo, and *gotra* means the family and race of Buddha. The meaning commonly presented in their Sanskrit words as the original words corresponding to Buddha-nature is the possibility-of-becoming-Buddha. See Ogawa Ichijo, *Hodokesho Siso* (Tokyo: Humieido Publication, 1976), 24-6.
34. Frank Reynolds, Hegel Revisited: "A History of Religions/ Buddhist Studies Perspective," in *AAR Nineteenth Century Theology Group 1992*, 109.
35. Hodgson, Hodgson, "Logic, History, and Alternative Paradigms in Hegel's Interpretation of the Religions," in *AAR Nineteenth Century Theology Group* 1992, 75.
36. Yu-hui Chen, *Abolutes Nichts und rhythmisches Sein* (Berlin: Bamberg University, 1999), 147. Translation is mine.
37. Hodgson, *Winds of the Spirit: A Constructive Christian theology* (Louisville, Kentucky: Westminster John Knox Press, 1994), 106-7.
38. David R. Griffin, "Buddhist Thought and Whitehead's Philosophy," *International Philosophical Quarterly* 14 (1974): 262-84.
39. Criticizing Hegelian systematic idea, Kierkegaard says "the systematic idea is the identity of subject and object, the unity of thought and being. The corresponds in an equally abstract-objective thought has no relation to the existing subject; and while we are always confronted with the difficult question of how the existing subject slips into this objectivity." See Kierkegaard, "Concluding Unscientific Postscript to the 'Philosophical Fragments'" in *A Kierkegaard Anthology*, ed. Robert Brentall (Princeton: Princeton University Press, 1973) 205.

Chapter Two

Creativity and God in Process

In his book *Christianity and Process Thought*, Joseph Bracken examines Christianity in the contemporary world. Bracken shows how the Christian tradition adapts the Whiteheadian process model in which the church transforms itself constantly in an organic relationship with the world. On the basis of Whitehead's process thought, he closely reinterprets divine and human creativity, the contrasting concept of good and evil, the church and the kingdom of God, divine providence and human freedom, the almightiness of God. In particular, Bracken is deeply concerned with where God does exist in the midst of evil arising in our society and how the divine reality revealed in the triune God ultimately transforms the power of evil to that of good. "God as a community of divine persons" is not an abstract but concrete God who is deeply engaged in all the elements of which the world is made. Bracken, in accordance with the Whiteheadian view of God, discusses how the Kingdom of God specifically envisages the feature of its goodness in the dynamic situation of our life world. He also examines the problem of human freedom in the midst of divine ongoing providence and explores time in eternity, which constantly both creates and limits human freedom in the continuum of the past-present-future.

Bracken adopts Whitehead's notion of creativity in his explanation of the triune God. Whitehead's creativity is that disjunctive diversities (the Father, the Son, and the Spirit) become a complex unity (God) and vice versa. Explaining the triadic structure of the divine reality in terms of Whitehead's creativity, Bracken argues that creativity is inseparable from the divine nature. "Creativity is not a reality independent of God but a reality within God. It is the inner nature or basic principle of existence and activity for God."[1] God constitutes God-self through creative process. For Bracken, therefore, creativity is the inner nature of God, and this is why he insists that God is not only one person but also described as the divine community of three persons by adapting into his theological perspective Whitehead's principle of creativity that "many become one and are increased by one."[2]

Bracken's view of God and creativity, in my opinion, does not fully reflect Whiteheadian God and creativity. In Bracken's view, Whiteheadian God's initial aim plays a very important role in explaining that all evil power finally can be transformed to the power of good. According to Bracken, God's initial aim is always the right direction toward which the world should proceed. All evil features in the world originate from creatures' spontaneity in which they can be outside the vision of God. In this way, disorder is brought into the cosmic process of the world. Bracken thus says, "Here I would argue that, when and if such mindless evil happens, it is due to the misguided decision of the creature."[3] Bracken sharply contrasts "good" with "evil" in the cosmic process of the world. In other words, the evil occurring in the world originates in the creature's turning away from divine plan or God's initial aim, whereas the good comes from our responding to God's persuasion in a proper way and then following divine plan. "They do not order us to do what they want but instead seek to persuade us to do what is right through what Whitehead calls divine 'initial aims.'"[4] Divine initial aim is patient and enduring by giving the human community a new focus on His/Her plan and ultimately drawing the kingdom of God on earth.[5]

However, I doubt that Whitehead intended Bracken's view through his notion of God and creativity. I would argue that Whitehead's concept of creativity contains in its meaning the unceasing interaction between two opposite characters—order and disorder, cosmos and chaos, good and evil, and so forth: one cannot exist without the other. This means that those two opposites are complementary rather than contradictory in Whitehead's concept of creativity. They are cyclically revolved and transformed by each other, so that the opposites constantly produce "novelty" in their multilateral relationship rather than that one proceeds unilaterally toward the other, i.e., a certain final goal such as the kingdom of God or the Universal Community.

Bracken, of course, mentions the non-separable relation between good and evil. Explaining the collective powers of good and evil, he says that "all human communities are a mixture of good and evil; hence, each of them contributes by its mode of operation to the collective power of evil as well as to the collective power of good in this world."[6] Such a collective power of evil is associated with the group identity. "The members of a given community have a very strong influence on one another's attitudes and behavior."[7] In other words, although one is involved in a certain group with his or her good purpose, he or she often tends to uncritically follow the group's direction, which might have the negative spirit or hostility "toward nonmembers or rival groups."[8]

Bracken, however, discusses the good-evil interaction only at the level of the human community. For Bracken, creativity is the process of transforming "the various distorted forms of human community"[9] into the goodness of God's kingdom. "In the end, then, awareness of the ongoing coexistence of the collective power of good and of evil in this world should make us humble in assessing our own contribution to the coming of God's kingdom."[10] In other words, God's kingdom, the Universal Community is the ultimate end "for good in this end unfettered from the hybrid of good and evil."

This understanding of the Universal Community is closer to the Hegelian concept of Absolute Spirit than to the Whiteheadian concept of God and creativity. For Hegel, the lower category is partly transformed and preserved at the level of higher category, and the contradiction of opposite elements (e.g., good and evil) are dissolved in their synthesis. Hegel insists that two opposite predicates are synthesized in a higher status where they reconcile and transcend all of the contrasting categories toward the Absolute Spirit without any contradiction. Bracken states that "provided that we continue to love the person of Jesus and what he stands for in terms of the collective power of good, we are still on the way to salvation for ourselves and those around us."[11] His concept of the collective power of good is compared to Hegelian Absolute Spirit, which has no tension with evil.

Yet, dynamic tension between the opposites is a great source of creativity in Whitehead's process. Rather the positive contrast brings novelty by way of concrescence and transition. The one-many relationship in Whitehead's concept of creativity exemplifies such a paradox. Whitehead's creativity does not mean that the many proceed toward the one final reality but that the many becomes the one and vice versa in a cyclical movement.

According to Whitehead, concrescence is described as a "micro-cosmic process" in which an actual entity is developed and forms itself as a particular being in relationship with other actual entities.[12] In Whitehead's view, the universe is composed of all actual entities in the process of acting and becoming. He identifies "final realities" as "actual entities" or "actual occasions." At one moment a being is embodied and is an actual entity, which is distinguished from an eternal object participating in a being in that moment. According to Whitehead,

> Actual entities are the final real things of which the world is made up. There is no going behind actual entities to find anything more real. They differ among themselves: God is an actual entity. And so is the most trivial puff of existence in far-off empty space. But though there are gradations of importance, and diversities of function, yet in the principles which actuality exemplifies all are on the same level. The final facts are, all alike, actual entities; and these actual entities are drops of experience, complex and interdependent.[13]

These complex and interdependent experiences are formed by the continuous current of process, which is the event of creativity in which an actual entity realizes itself concretely. Whitehead opposes the substantial view in which a fixed and unchangeable reality supports the phenomenal world. Instead, he understands reality as process constituted by a stream.

This process vision is concretely developed by concrescence and transition; the former is the internal process of becoming of an actual entity, and the latter means that a complete actual entity gives its data to other actual entities for their new concrescence. These two notions elucidate the process in which many or diversity becomes one or unity.

Concrescence indicates that the disjunctive "many" through transition is transformed into a new unity, which has its own unique features through "final cause."[14] At this point, the disjunctive "many" participate in the process, forming a new unity. They make an actual occasion in a moment when various kinds of entities are "together," so that "many" coexist in a new entity, which has its own unique features through "final cause."[15] At this point the disjunctive 'many' participate in the process forming a new unity and make an actual occasion in a moment when various kinds of entities are "together."

This process of concrescence is distinctively different from the Hegelian Absolute Spirit because the one unity attained by the process of concrescence is constantly open to the many. When an actual entity attains its completion with its unique features by the process of concrescence, the entity continuously participates in the constitution of 'many.' As such a completed entity offers itself as data for other actual entities and participates in the formation of new entities. Whitehead calls this process "transition."[16] According to Whitehead, transition is the macrocosmic process that moves from particular existent to particular existent.[17]

For Whitehead, concrescence and transition are shaped by "final cause" and "efficient cause." Thomas E. Hosinski describes Whitehead's view of final cause and efficient cause as follows:

> Efficient causation expresses the transition from actual entity to actual entity, while final causation expresses how each actual entity individually becomes itself. Efficient causation describes how the actual entity as 'superject'—that is, 'perished,' drained of subjective immediacy—yet lives on its future to affect a new concrescing occasion. Final causation describes the process of superjective self-creation, based on the process of transition to the future (the superject). There are these two types of "process": transition (from one actual entity to another) concrescence (development within one actual entity). Efficient causation concerns transition: final causation concerns concrescence. Both are there in the 'final real facts' of our experience.[18]

While final cause means self-formation in which a novel entity forms its unique characteristics by making its own subjective decision, efficient cause indicates the influence of 'many' by which a novel unity is formed. Thus, these two types of process are interrelated. That is to say, a would-be novel entity has its own subjective purpose by final cause, selects 'many' according to its own purpose, and completes its unique characteristics, which are made up of concrescence. Also, when the novel entity is completed, it offers itself as data for the constitution of other actual entities. At this point, an actual entity offering itself functions as efficient cause, which is the process of transition.

For Whitehead, actual entities, in the process of concrescence and transition, constitute themselves in relationship with others by experience. Actual entity is the acting and experiencing being. Activity means experiencing, receiving, and including other entities. "Every experiencing subject can become an object for some other experiencing subject."[19] We experience other objects and are influenced by others through concrescence and transition.

Thus, the process of becoming is the process of experiencing. By way of concrescence, this process of becoming is the process of acting, which receives and transforms other objects into a definite unity. Whitehead writes that "concrescence is the name for the process in which the universe of many things acquires an individual unity in a determinate relegation of each item of the 'many' to its subordination in the constitution of the novel 'one.'"[20] In terms of concrescence, the term 'thing,' or 'entity' means 'one' among 'many' realized and decided in the process of concrescence. In other words, thing, or entity is individual entity in the process of concrescence where one becomes many and many becomes one. Thus, thing or entity always exists in interrelationship with other objects in the process of becoming.

The experience of an actual entity formed in concrescence is the experiencing of other objects. Experiencing does not mean that objects are reflected only in an experiencing subject but that they intervene in the subject and constitute the subject itself. Whitehead calls the principle of the experience based on subject-object interrelationship "reformed subjectivist principle,"[21] which means that subject cannot exist without object and vice versa. Our experiences are possible only when we are related to objectified data. We ourselves are experiencing beings in which objects are always immanent. I as subject am interrelated with others as objects in concrescence. According to Whitehead, concrescence process in the process of experience in which I form my unique subject in relationship with object. Subject-object interrelationship in my experience means intermingling other objects with my subject. Whitehead writes the following as to experience based on subject-object relationship:

The occasion as subject has a 'concern' for the object. And the 'concern' at once places the object as a component in the experience of the subject, with an affective tone drawn from this object and directed towards it. With this interpretation the subject-object relation is the fundamental structure of experience. . . . The process of experiencing is constituted by the reception of entities, whose being is antecedent to that process, into the complex fact which is that process itself. These antecedent entities, thus received as factors into the process of experiencing, are terms 'objects' for that experiential occasion. Thus primarily the terms 'object' expresses the relation of the entity, thus denoted, to one or more occasions of experiencing.[22]

Concrescence is the element of internal constitution in an actual occasion based on the subject-object interrelationship of our experiences. All actual entities are developed of concrescence, which is constituted by experiences. Our experiences are always in process by which all actual entities are interrelated by the function of concrescence

Therefore, the one as unity through the process of concrescence does not mean the one as opposed to evil. Rather it means a complex unity. Whitehead says that "the many components of a complex datum have a unity: this unity is a 'contrast of entities.'"[23] In other words, the creative advance in the one-many dynamic relation is made by proceeding "from 'contrasts' to 'contrasts of contrasts,'" which does not mean proceeding to the ultimate end but "indefinitely to higher grades of contrasts."[24] If we follow this position of Whitehead, creative advance does not refer to mass movements toward only good but rather to ceaseless contrasts of contrasts in which good and evil are constantly intermingled in the journey toward a complex unity.

From Whitehead's perspective, God's initial aim or purpose is in the process of concrescence and transition in its interaction with the world. It is always exposed to the possibility of change and transformation in time; the Father's initial aim is potential reality from God's unconditioned conceptual prehension of eternal objects. God's initial aims are supplemented and developed by God's consequent nature, showing how God is affected by and responds to the temporal actual world. It is hard to find God's consequent nature (which Whitehead also emphasizes as well as God's primordial nature) in Bracken's argument of God, which focuses too much on God's initial aim. He writes that "since we creatures do not always respond to the divine initial aim as we should, and bad things happen as a result."[25]

Yet, divine initial aim cannot be conceived of without its creative process in the world. Divine initial aim cannot be defined without considering its contextual situations. It remains as "pure potentiality" without being intermingled with the world. Under Whitehead's principle of creativity, divine initial aim and consequent nature cannot be thought of independently. In other words, we cannot simply say that bad things happen because we do not follow divine initial aim. Divine initial aim can have its limits in a complicated circumstance. It cannot be the absolute standard to judge either good or bad. It can result in bad things or good things according to its application. For instance, Jesus' message that "I am the way, the truth, and the life" (John 14:6, NRSV) is composed of abstract nouns (the way, the truth, the life) is a good example of divine initial aim. "The way, the truth, and the life" should be answered in our life context. A question is what it means to follow such a divine initial aim. Do bad things happen if we do not follow the message of those abstract nouns? What is important is how to interpret the divine message and apply it to our life context. In this situation if we define Jesus as the way, the truth, and the life in a parochial view, bad things may happen although we can argue that we follow the divine initial aim. Further, "No one comes to the Father except through me" (Jesus) as a divine initial aim can be applied to an exclusive attitude to other religious figures (Muhammad, Buddha, or Confucius), whereby religious conflicts may always happen in our world.

From Whitehead's perspective, therefore, the truth is always to an open process. Bracken also points out that

> all truth is the expression of someone's subjective experience of reality and contributes to the formation of a new objective reality, which will be open to interpretation by a new set of truth-seekers, a new set of actual occasions or momentary subjects of experience consciously or unconsciously in search of the truth.[26]

In this sense, Bracken highlights "truth-intersubjectivity" by way of which people make a dialogue with others and learn one another's perspective toward a broader horizon of truth. Bracken identifies this broader horizon of truth with a common ground: "As this common ground becomes ever broader in scope, people instinctively feel that they are closer to the full truth and objectivity of the issue under discussion."[27] I agree that we become closer to the truth and gain more common ground by learning other perspectives. Yet, I would have to argue that such a common ground is also posited in a ceaseless path towards the creative advance in which the one and the many are intermingled. In other words, Whitehead's process vision does not assume the kingdom of God or the Universal Community formed only in the convergence or common ground. Bracken argues, however, that

> all these overlapping communities of interpretation then converge to form the Universal Community, which corresponds to the kingdom of God on earth.

... Rather it is the unanimity achieved through our mutual recognition of interconnected partial standpoints, all of which contain some truth but none of which contains the whole truth.[28]

If so, a question is whether the unanimity contains the whole truth. Whitehead's process view never assumes that unanimity contains the whole truth.

The whole truth is the creative advance itself made by change and transformation. That is to say, the whole truth does not mean the common denominator of each partial standpoint. Rather it means that the part reflects the whole, while the whole is creatively transformed in organic relation to other new entities (i.e., culture or tradition). This recognition of the whole truth is very important, especially in inter-religious dialogue. I agree with Bracken's argument that "real progress will be made here only if the participants recognize not only the relative character of the truth claims of other religions but also the relative character of the truth claims of their own religion." All the truth claims should be able to relativize themselves in a new dimension of a broader horizon. As Bracken says, a religious tradition does not represent the whole truth: "this is not to say that the truth claims proper to one's own religion are false or untrue, but only that they do not represent the whole truth about ultimate reality, whether ultimate reality be conceived as a personal God or as an impersonal cosmic force."[29] His recognition of the truth manifested in each religion apparently entails the necessity of inter-religious dialogue in which one finds the weakness of the truth claim limited to one's own tradition and experience and learns other religious traditions and experiences, as one moves toward a greater horizon of the truth. Knowing always expands its horizons in relation to other horizons and differences in the process of becoming.

However, a question may be raised in relation to the view of the truth shown in Bracken's religious pluralism: Is the whole truth understood as the truth attained by the addition of each portion of the truth according to the Euclidean method? From the Whiteheadian view of creativity developed in the non-Euclidean way, the part is in the whole and vice versa. To put it another way, each religious context shows only the facts and values limited to its context, but refers to the whole that makes multi-dimensional religious experiences converge. Since Buddhism does not speak only for itself but the whole world, we should be able to listen and learn its believers' truth through their eyes. That is to say, inter-religious dialogue is necessary not because each religious tradition is partially true but because each refers to the whole in its own terms. In this view, the part (each religious tradition) and the whole (the truth) are cyclically revolved in the process of becoming.

NOTES

1. Joseph A. Bracken, S.J. *Christianity and Process Thought: Spirituality for a Changing World* (Philadelphia: Templeton Foundation Press, 2006), 19.
2. Alfred North Whitehead, *Process and Reality*, ed. David Ray Griffin & Donald W. Sherburne (New York: The Free Press, 1978), 18.
3. Bracken, *Christianity and Process Thought*, 32.
4. Ibid., 21.
5. Ibid., 29-32.
6. Ibid., 42.
7. Ibid., 58
8. Ibid., 44.
9. Ibid., 47.
10. Ibid., 51.
11. Ibid., 52.
12. Whitehead, *Process and Reality*, 214.
13. Whitehead, *Modes of Thought* (New York: The Free Press, 1968), 93.
14. Whitehead, *Process and Reality*, 212.
15. Ibid., 21.
16. Ibid., 210.
17. Ibid., 55.
18. Thomas E. Hosinski, *Stubborn Fact and Creative Advance: An Introduction to the Metaphysics of Alfred North Whitehead* (Lanham, Maryland: Rowman & Littlefield Publishers, Inc. 1993), 96.
19. Ibid., 42.
20. Whitehead, *Process and Reality*, 211
21. Ivor Leclerc, *Whitehead's metaphysics: An Introductory Exposition* (London: George Allen and Unwin Ltd., 1958), 116.
22. Whitehead, *Adventures of Ideas* (New York: The Free Press, 1993), 178.
23. Whitehead, *Process and Reality*, 36.
24. Ibid., 212.
25. Bracken, *Christianity and Process Thought*, 85.
26. Bracken, *Christianity and Process thought*, 68.
27. Ibid.
28. Ibid., 68-75.
29. Ibid., 76.

Chapter Three

Divine Paradox and Harmony in Whitehead and Jung

This chapter examines the love of God in paradox and harmony, a paradigm developed by both Whitehead and Carl Gustav Jung (1875-1961). Both develop their arguments in the correlation of the opposites—the subject and object, the conscious and the unconscious, God and the world, good and evil. From their perspectives, those opposites are not antagonistic but relational and thereby become the conditions of creative transformation. In this view, God's love is based on the paradoxical combination of the opposites in which love does not mean the massive movement toward goodness, but the transformational and comprehensive whole of the contradictories.

In this chapter, I discuss Whitehead's notion of prehension, whereby God and the world paradoxically prehend each other by being affected by and affecting each other. This process of God and the world are considered as creative ongoingness based on love. I explain this process of love by discussing the problem of Robert Neville's criticism of Whitehead's God and creativity.

This aspect of God's love is similarly shown in Jung's discussion of the conscious and the unconscious. I discuss Jung's divine love in the balance between opposites, i.e., the attunement of ego-consciousness with the depth of unconsciousness. I recognize that this exemplification of God's love is made in the paradoxical combination of Jung's divine quaternity.

By comparing the perspectives of Whitehead with Jung on divine love, I show how they critically overcome the problem of Aristotle's Law of Contrast. Both Whitehead and Jung emphasize non-sensory perception (causal efficacy or the collective unconscious), which makes the non-separable relation between God and the world. I argue that through this relation all the joys and sufferings of the world are immanent in divine reality while God transforms such immanence and realizes God's nature of love in creativity.

WHITEHEAD

Whitehead insists that actual entities as "final realities" constituting the world uphold their values in their relationship with others and the whole universe. Through their value-realization all actual entities are in the process of creative advance.[1]

To avoid the traditional subject-object dualism, Whitehead presents two perceptive modes of actual entities, "causal efficacy" and "presentational immediacy." While causal efficacy is unconscious perception, presentational immediacy is consciously clear perception.[2] These two modes of feeling cannot be separated from each other, making an actual entity "relational self" in the process of becoming.

This relational self becomes the foundation of love in which the subject and the object are interrelated. Love is based on the relation initiated by feeling through causal efficacy and presentational immediacy. God's love is engaged in the enjoyments of all actual entities. In this engagement God intensifies the harmony of the opposites in creative advance.

Therefore, love is creative activity, which means activity that does not control but instead persuades and transforms through the feeling of unification in multiplicity. Although this feeling is caused by the multiplicity of data, those data are perceived as a single and definite feeling through the process of concrescence and transition.[3] In this process, all actual entities influence one another by prehension (i.e., perception or feeling), the process by which an actual entity relates or reacts to its environment. Every actual entity responds to the influence of its environment and transforms its environment for its own sake.[4]

An actual entity's experience is "feeling arising out of the realization of contrast under identity."[5] The depth of an actual entity's feeling-intensity is enhanced by the process of contrast which brings unity-in-diversity and diversity-in-unity. An actual entity has value for its own sake by increasing the intensity of "satisfaction" in the process of concrescence. An actual entity also has value for others by providing data for subsequent actual entities in the process of transition.[6]

This view of prehension in concrescence and transition becomes a foundation for understanding "the expression of divine love for the world"[7] as creative activity. According to John Cobb and David Griffin,

> God's creative love extends to all the creatures. The promotion of enjoyment is God's primary concern throughout the whole process of creative evolution. . . . God wants us *all* to enjoy. . . . Accordingly, God wants our enjoyment to increase the enjoyments of others.[8]

Our world is based on the transmission of feelings, which intensifies aesthetic experiences. In particular, God's love is all-embracing love promoting the aesthetic formation by concrescing the contrasting elements in prehension. God and the world affect and respond to each other in their aesthetic feeling.

According to Donald Sherburne, aesthetic feeling "adds a dimension of extra significance to experience: experience is significance, and extra significance is richness of experience."[9] God is the source of novelty, which brings richness of experience to the world. God's creativity is the activity that transforms a multiplicity of data into "the one rich experience." God incorporates all of our joys and sufferings in divine reality and conducts creative acts toward the betterment of the world.

According to Whitehead, "God is that element in virtue of which our purposes extend beyond values for ourselves to values for others. God is that element in virtue of which the attainment of such a value for others transforms itself into value for ourselves."[10] God's love is in the extension of values for all. God works for all the value-realizations and enjoyments of actual entities in love and order. However, "excessive order can inhibit enjoyment."[11] Order is initially formed in God's primordial nature as God's purpose with respect to the temporal world. God provides the world with order by preferentially adopting eternal objects as principles.[12]

This order is not fixed but continues to be transformed in relation to the world, so that it is directed toward enjoyment for all actual entities. This character of order "must not be lost, but it also must not be dominant."[13] Divine order contains the possibility of change in its existence, which performs "the art of progress." "The art of progress is to preserve order amid change, and to preserve change amid order."[14] Change amid order is conducted in God's consequent nature in which God is influenced by and responds to the temporal actual world. By way of God's consequent nature, God's order is interfused with creative love, which is concerned with the enjoyment of all. In the circular movement of order and love, "God's purpose in the creative advance is the evocation of intensities."[15] In such intensities, God and creativity are not separable in God's love. Because creativity itself is the expression of love, God constitutes God-self in love and creativity.

In this sense I do not agree with Robert Neville's interpretation that the Whiteheadian God is not identified with creativity. According to Neville, "God, in Whitehead's view, is not at all to be identified with creativity, but is itself a unique creature."[16] Neville divides creativity into ontological and cosmological creativity. Cosmological creativity is "exercised by creatures constituting the world."[17] According to Neville, "Whitehead's creativity is this cosmological creativity."[18] The cosmological creativity is "contingent upon God's ontological creativity."[19]

In Whitehead's philosophic system, however, one cannot expect to understand all elements constituting the universe by separating some from others. Instead, he views all beings as mutually interrelated in an organic system. John Berthrong writes,

> Whitehead does not suggest that one can separate any one item, even an abstract Notion like creativity, from another except where the mutual standpoints are separate.... Creativity is not some kind of ontological surd free floating without connection to anything else in the Whiteheadian cosmos. If this is the case, then we must seek to find a way to reunite God and creativity.[20]

Because one cannot understand God without creativity, creativity cannot be understood without God. God and creativity are the ultimate powers for bringing the normative principle to dynamic actualities. Even if the two are distinguished in their notions, God and creativity are intrinsically linked into a whole.

Whitehead's non-separation between God and creativity can be understood in terms of God's love, which is creative activity itself. "To act in love is to act with creation; to act against love is to act against creation."[21] God's love is the creative power, which is not substantial but relational. God's love is based on the relational nature, continuously emerging in creative process to transform both good and evil.

Therefore, I identify another problem in Neville's argument that Whitehead reduces God into an actual entity "as a being among other beings."[22] Whitehead defines God as an actual entity but, unlike other actual entities, not as an actual occasion (a temporal actual entity). Also, because Whitehead's notion of actual entity is based on relational nature, it is problematic to understand that Whitehead's God has a reductive character.

Whitehead's God concerns the creative transformation of contradictory elements such as chaos and order, good and evil in the relational paradigm. The maximum depth of the correlation between these contradictions performs divine love and harmony.[23] God's love is the expression of harmony realized in creative activity. God's creative love builds the organic relationship of the universe.

From Whitehead's perspective, order and chaos are complementary, not antagonistic. Both elements are necessary for the aesthetic enjoyment in creativity. Chaos is the source for bringing the higher type of order through the contrast of contrasts. God's love is the activity that transforms "order and chaos" into creative advance to promote well-being and enjoyment for all. For Whitehead, therefore, good and evil, and joy and suffering are relative and temporary. They become interchanged in the process of concrescence and transition. While immersed in this process, God's love (with order) contributes to promoting the satisfaction of all by bringing the contradictory elements into the intensity of their correlation and transformation.

JUNG

Whitehead's key notion of God-in-creativity is compared to Jung's notion of the collective unconscious. Steve Odin writes, "Jung reassigns the divine faculties and cosmological roles to the collective unconscious at the depths of the psyche; thus God is fully immanent in each occasion of experience."[24] Jung's collective unconsciousness refers to the deepest layer of the human unconsciousness, which is present at birth and greatly influences one's psyche in various ways without being recognized by one's consciousness. The collective unconscious is shaped a priori and reveals universal phenomena throughout all humankind beyond time and space. For Jung, the divine is experienced through the medium of the collective unconscious. According to Odin, "Whitehead's dipolar nature of God is virtually identified with each occasion of experience, and so God is comprehended as the transpersonal and (collective) unconscious dimensions of each event."[25]

Jung argues that from the strictly empirical point of view, it is wholly impossible to distinguish manifestations of God (divine love, spiritual vision) from the unconscious psyche. "It is only through the psyche that we can establish that God acts upon us, but we are unable to distinguish whether these actions come from God or from the unconscious. We cannot tell whether God and the unconscious are actually two different entities."[26]

For Jung, the religious self is developed not only by ego-consciousness, but also by the archetypal images, the images of a-priori forms through which we experience God. The God-image is formed in the archetypal process of the self. In this way we cannot separate God from the unconscious self in the depth of the psyche.

From Jung's perspective, God is not described as a transcendent reality in a dualistic structure between God and the world. God is God-within-the-human-mind. Yet, Jung's argument concerning God is distinguishable from the idea that God is produced by individual psychic phenomenon.[27] Jung relates God to his notion of the collective unconscious of the mind, which is beyond the personal dimension of the mind. Jung defines the divine character in relation to the universal and collective dimension of the mind. The image of God through the unconscious represents the wholeness encompassing the contrasting poles of good and evil in their compensatory relationship.[28]

In this sense divine love is based on the holistic image, which incorporates opposite elements in the relational self. Christ represents the image of the relational self. According to Jung, we cannot describe the wholeness of Christ-image only with trinity. The element of devil should be added to the image of Christ in order to express the integration of the opposites.[29] Jung's argument about the complementary relation between good and evil through the symbol of "quaternity" instead of the trinity signifies that God reveals wholeness through the relativism of opposites, which are transformed by their compensatory relation.[30] For Jung, the opposite element of good and evil is not substantial but relational and transformative. The holistic image of Christ manifests the correlation of contradictory factors in the balance between the conscious and the unconscious.

In particular, in his work *Answer to Job* (1952), Jung develops his view of God with his theological insight of good and evil. In contrast to traditional theism, Jung defines God as the source of both good and evil, which is also identified with the archetype from the collective unconscious. Jung applies this relative character of good and evil to his notion of God in relation to the divine unconscious. For Jung, good and evil are in a compensatory relation by way of which divine unconsciousness stores the correlative features of all the opposites. The ambivalent character of both good and evil is formed in the divine unconsciousness, which converges with the depth of the human unconsciousness. According to Jung, the unconscious is the medium connecting the divine and the human mind, thereby promoting the creative transformation of contradictory poles. "Because the unconscious is the matrix mind, the quality of creativeness attaches to it."[31]

God cannot be separated from the unconscious self. God is creatively associated with the human mind through the transformation of consciousness and unconsciousness. God is described as the richness of the symbolic contents in the Self from the human experience of the divine. The Self is the center of the human mind symbolically incorporating the conscious and the unconscious. People project the image of God formed in the Self onto an external object. Thus, God is originally "the God-within,"[32] which is formed in the deep layer of the mind. The God-within does not mean the subjective inner experience of the psyche but rather the divine experience rooted in the archetype that is collectively formed.

Given this archetypal form, Jung's view of God is not simply based on the subjective image, but also on the subjective-objective images formed in the process of the collective unconsciousness. God as the collective unconscious is the holistic feature of the Self, which attempts to recover all dissociated fragments at the expense of the one-sided ego-process. This empirical aspect of God in the archetypal Self cannot be simply attributed to the subjective experience of the inner-psyche.

According to Jung, this religious experience is involved in the individuation process of the self, conducted by deriving the image of God from archetypal vision. "Individuation means becoming an in-dividual," and, in so far as 'in-dividuality' embraces our innermost, last, and incomparable uniqueness, it also implies becoming one's own self."[33] In the individuation process one might face the problem of how to nurture one's relationship with other selves and other values systems. Jung's solution to this problem is to draw the collective unconscious into the individuation process so that one overcomes the limitations of the ego-consciousness by incorporating the inner depth of the collective unconscious, which is beyond personal value. In other words, the individuation process is a self-realization in association with the environment, or collective.

The image of Christ is based on the perfect model of this individuation and thereby embraces the opposite elements in his love. This means that divine love opens hearts to a new dimension of experience arising in the unconscious. Divine love is based on wholeness which combines a new dimension of highly personalized experiences that are not confined in traditional symbolic forms. Jung's depth of psychic nature becomes the power for transforming and overcoming the limited character of ego-consciousness. "The images of wholeness offered by the unconscious"[34] become the basis of love in Jung's depth psychology.

A COMPARISON BETWEEN WHITEHEAD AND JUNG ON THE LOVE OF GOD

From Whitehead's and Jung's perspectives, we can define God's love in the intensity of harmony between the opposite elements. True and false are both aspects of a single entity in the paradigms of Whitehead and Jung. The opposite elements of good and evil, order and chaos, God and the world are not independent realities but the complementary characters in an organic relation. They are not static in the dualistic way of true and false, but always changed and transformed by the continuous cycle of true and false.

From both perspectives, the pattern of harmony and order is formed in the ceaseless increase of the dynamic circle of true and false or good and evil. The state of harmony or order is reached not by eliminating paradox but by drawing on the paradoxical combination of the opposites.

Of course, although they are complementary in their perspectives, there is a difference between the paradigms of Whitehead and Jung. While Jung includes both good and evil in the divine, Whitehead's notion of God concerns the realization of the goodness and order in the ongoing creative process.[35] For Whitehead, evil does not exist in God's nature but emerges in the finite embodiments of creativity, which are also transformational in God's creative love.

On the other hand, Jung incorporates all contradictory elements in the divine archetype and the collective unconscious. While Whitehead describes the divine harmony between the opposites in the process of becoming, Jung accentuates the unity of the opposites in the archetype, the a priori form of the mind. While Whitehead's divine love is formed in the creative advance, which makes harmony between the opposites in the process of becoming, Jung's divine love is realized in the representation of archetype that already constitutes the unity of the opposite elements.

Despite these differences, however, I find similarities in the divine love developed by Whitehead and Jung. Their approaches take an insider's view rather than an outsider's. According to Jung, divine love is not a love that is shackled in the creed or doctrine of one's own tradition but is instead one that is open to a new dimension of religious experience arising in the manifestations of the (collective) unconscious. The doctrine of trinity exemplifies an outsider's view ascribing diverse religious values and models to a unified pattern. The doctrine of trinity cannot reflect the whole of individual religious experiences. Jung's argument about divine quaternity stems from being immersed in personal experiences from an insider's view. God's love is not only beyond any doctrinal system, but also embodied in all diverse forms of religious activities and experiences.

In a similar manner, Whitehead's notion of creativity is understood as an insider's view. This view focuses on the diversity of the divine in creativity, rather than driving the divine reality into a unified whole (through dogma) because all church dogma is also in the process of becoming. Differences are not antagonistic but contributable elements to the creative relations. "[Whitehead]'s God is not an external being who 'encounters' from without, or who cannot be experienced at all but only believed in. Rather, God is experienced, usually unconsciously, or the borderlands between conscious and unconscious awareness."[36] God's love is always conducted in this empirical process, showing the divine character immersed in the world. In this process God affects and is affected by the world through internal relationship between actual entities.

The problem with Aristotle's logic is that it is exercised only from the outsider's point of view in which differences are reduced into one unified system of logic. Paradox is regarded as pathological in this logical system. But for Whitehead and Jung, paradox results from the correlation of diverse phenomena in different contexts. Whereas Aristotle's logic aims to eliminate such a paradoxical situation, Whitehead and Jung regard it as the element enriching the process of concrescence or individuation, whereby God's love is accomplished through the correlation between the opposites.

God's love through the balance between the opposites is based on the symbolic formation of religious images and concepts. According to Jung, if symbols are understood and analyzed within the framework of logical consistency, they can lose their meanings and values.[37] Divine symbols attain their deeper significance and value by the way the unknown world is mediated to our life. To put it another way, the divine symbol is beyond the dualistic distinction of the rational and irrational through the encounter of our conscious with the unknown. In this sense divine love is understood not as literal but as symbolic, thus enabling the divine to become interrelated with our life-world.

God's love has neither any meanings nor any effect in a state of dissociation between the two different realms, the unconscious and conscious. God's love through various forms of religious symbols cannot be understood within the bound of sensory perception. Sensory perception is the medium of conveying the meaning of divine symbols to the perceiver. In other words, sensory perception does not completely grasp the whole content and meaning of the divine symbol, so Jung seeks the validity of non-sensory perception in understanding the divine symbol.

Affirming nonsensory perception in his explanation of postmodern theology, David Griffin writes that "postmodern theology's recognition of nonsensory perception allows for a dimension or element of perceptual experience that is not a product of culturally conditioned frameworks and is therefore common to us all."[38] Nonsensory perception cannot be explained in the mechanistic model ruled by dualism and materialism. Griffin continues to say,

> At the root of the modern worldview, along with the sensationist doctrine of perception, was the mechanistic idea of nature. This mechanistic idea of natural entities forced most modern minds to choose between dualism and materialism, both of which are extremely problematic. Dualism left the modern mind unable to explain its relation to its body; materialism led the modern mind to deny itself.[39]

In the mechanistic model, mind and nature, the subject and the object, and God and the world are separated from each other. Each of them is an independent substance and material dominated by causality.

Symbolic meaning and effect are the keys to understand the significance of nonsensory perception. The meaning of symbols cannot be understood within the bound of sensory perception. Sensory perception is, of course, the medium of conveying the meaning of symbols to the perceiver. As Morris

Philipson indicates the significance of sensory perception, "the symbol, thus, is part of an attempt to link a given known with an unknown; it is a content, available to sensory perception which would connect present experience with something that is not immediately available."[40] In other words, sensory perception should function as a medium to transmit something directly unavailable. Sensory perception does not completely grasp the whole content and meaning of the symbol.

In this context of symbolic meaning, Jung brings the significance of non-sensory perception into his discussion of synchronicity. With the notion of synchronicity, Jung attempts to show the archetypal process of the human psyche, which is driven from the a-priori form or primordial image deeply rooted in human unconsciousness. Jung articulates that the depth of the psyche is closely connected with an outer event through the synchronistic moment. Jung's theory of synchronicity is an attempt to theorize the non-causal dimension of the human experience irreducible to the cause-effect system of mind and nature. Jung argues that the correspondence of the inner psyche to the outer event is performed by the archetypal representation derived from the collective unconscious beyond the individual self. In this manner the synchronistic phenomenon cannot be properly described by the causal relation between mind and nature according to traditionally-Western logical reasoning.

Jung finds the value of the synchronistic phenomenon in its symbolic meaning, which he believes achieves the wholeness of the self or the union of the opposites. The symbolic meaning cannot be verified within the level of sensory perception. Given this understanding of synchronicity, Jung appeals to the non-sensory process of archetypal imagination (or representation) for delineating its symbolic meaning system.

Whitehead also shows nonsensory perception through his concepts of causal efficacy and presentational immediacy. Whitehead writes that

> causal efficacy is the hand of the settled past in the formation of the present. The sense data must therefore play a double role in perception. In the mode of presentational immediacy they are projected to exhibit the contemporary world in its spatial relations. In the mode of causal efficacy they exhibit the almost instantaneously precedent bodily organs as imposing their characters on the experience in question.[41]

For Whitehead, symbolic reference is composed of those two modes of perception. Symbolic reference is "the organic functioning whereby there is a transition from the symbol of the meaning."[42] In other words, symbolic reference might be considered the modes of combination between causal efficacy and presentational immediacy. Causal efficacy, causally inherited from the immediate past, is very dim and obscure. This is the primitive perception or prehension occurring in the initial phase of concrescence as "re-enactive" or "conformal" feeling. This mode of prehension is based not on conscious perception but on some "viscera" perception, which is closely associated with bodily or unconscious feeling in the experience of actual entities.

On the other hand, presentational immediacy refers to the spatio-temporal relation of our present sense-perception, which brings the present vivid consciousness.[43] For example, when I feel God's love through the cross, this feeling can only be my presentational description with its spatial presentation. Although vague, however, the cross as symbolic representation draws divine love into the abyss of being, surrounding my mind and body. This vagueness signifies that the cross is already transferred into my bodily or unconscious feeling, i.e., viscera perception before my spatial presentational immediacy.

With his notion of prehension, Whitehead sharply criticizes Hume's theory of perception by arguing that Hume concentrates only upon subjective sensory-perception and overlooks the aspect of causal efficacy.[44] In this sense Whitehead finds the value of the human experience in the midway between the subject and the object, wherein the perceiver contains both aspects of the subjective and the objective. In other words, the subjective experience is based on sensory perception whereas the objective experience refers to non-sensory perception. All past experiences indicate the objective side while the conscious perception of the present constitutes the subjective side. For Whitehead, just as the past is not separated from the present, so the objective and subjective are not separated through causal efficacy and presentational immediacy; our present experiences are not constituted in a clear cut of time but in the duration of time.

Both Whitehead and Jung contribute to the concept of love by their insights of perceptive modes (the conscious/unconscious or presentational immediacy/causal efficacy). These are the foundation of non-dualism between God and the world, or the subject and object. Although they seem to be separated in our conscious knowledge (or presentational immediacy), they are bound up with each other in the process of unconscious (or in causal efficacy).

God's love as understood by Whitehead and Jung is based on wholeness within particularistic diversity. The traditional systems of religious expression such as ritual and doctrinal forms are the objectified systems vis-à-vis one's personalized truth. They are deeply associated with many individuals' experiences of God's love over the ages but cannot fully reflect highly personalized religious experiences, which transform themselves through the process of concrescence or individuation.

God's love is manifested by being engaged in such individual circumstances. God's love is not the love developed by a fixed frame; it is the creative activity to transform and overcome the limited character of ego-consciousness. God's love paradoxically attunes different forms and values in a creative relation.

NOTES

1. Whitehead, *Process and Reality*, 18. Without the gradation of values, all actual entities are non-realities without definiteness. In this definiteness actual entities proceed to creative advance. See Whitehead, *Science and the Modern World* (New York: The Free Press, 1967), 93-4.

2. Whitehead, *Symbolism: Its Meaning and Effect* (New York: Fordham University Press, 1985), 42.

3. Whitehead, *Process and Reality*, 210-12.

4. Ibid., 35.

5. Whitehead, *Religion in the Making* (New York: Fordham University Press, 1996), 115.

6. Whitehead, *Process and Reality*, 26.

7. John Cobb and David Griffin, *Process Theology: An Introductory Exposition* (Philadelphia: The Westminster Press, 1976), 51.

8. Ibid., 56-7.

9. Donald Sherburne, *A Whiteheadian Aesthetic* (New Haven, NY: Yale University Press, 1961), 165.

10. Whitehead, *Religion in the Making* (New York: Fordham University Press, 1997), 158.

11. Cobb and Griffin, *Process Theology*, 59.

12. Whitehead, *Process and Reality*, 31-2, 344.

13. Cobb and Griffin, *Process Theology*, 59.

14. Whitehead, *Process and Reality*, 339.

15. Cobb and Griffin, *Process Theology*, 59.

16. Robert Neville, *Behind the Masks of God* (Albany, NY: SUNY, 1991), 60.

17. Robert C. Neville, *Creativity and God: A Challenge to Process Theology* (Albany, NY: SUNY, 1995), 8.

18. Robert Neville, *Behind the Masks of God*, 60.

19. Ibid.

20. John Berthrong, *Concerning Creativity: A Comparison of Chu Hsi, Whitehead, and Neville* (Albany, NY: SUNY, 1998), 85.

21. Majorie Hewitt Suchocki, *God Christ Church: A Practical Guide to Process Theology* (New York: Crossroad, 1989), 125.

22. Neville, *Behind the Masks of God*, 60.

23. Whitehead, *Adventures of Ideas* (New York: The Free Press, 19678), 284-95.

24. Steve Odin, *Process Metaphysics and Hua-yen Buddhism* (Albany, NY: SUNY, 1982), 159.

25. Ibid.

26. *The Collected Works of C.G. Jung*, trans. R.F.C. Hullmet, 2d ed., Bollingens Series, vol. 11, *Answer to Job* (Princeton, NJ: Princeton University Press, 1969), 468, hereafter referred to as *CW* with volume number of Jung's Collected Works.

27. Jung, *CW* 11, 58.

28. Jung, *Memories, Dreams, and Reflections*, ed. Aniela Jaffe, trans. Richard and Clara Winstor, (New York: Random House-Vintage Books, 1989), 329.

29. Jung, *CW* 11, 175.

30. Ibid., For Jung, quaternity is the symbol of the wholeness and also that of "God-within" dynamically developed in the human mind. In other words, God in our mind represents the wholeness including the antithetical images, whereby only trinitarian concepts of Father, Son, and Spirit cannot draw the whole image of God.

31. Jung, *CW* 11, 490.

32. Jung, *CW* 11, 58.

33. Jung, *CW* 7, 173.

34. Jung, *CW* 11, 469.

35. *Archetypal Process: Self and Divine in Whitehead, Jung, and Hillman*, ed., David Ray Griffin, (Evanston, Illinois: Northwestern University Press, 1989), 55.

36. Griffin, "Introduction," in *Archetypal Process*, 56.

37. Jung, CW 6, 474-5.

38. David Ray Griffin, *God& Religion in the Postmodern World: Essays in Postmodern Theology* (Albany, NY: SUNY, 1989), 4.

39. Ibid., 4-5.

40. Morris Philipson, *Outline of Jungian Aesthetics* (Evanston, IL: Northwestern University Press, 1963), 28.

41. Alfred North Whitehead, *Symbolism: Its Meaning and Effect* (New York: Fordham University Press, 1985), 50.

42. Ibid., 8.

43. Whitehead, *Process and Reality*, 118-23.

44. See Whitehead, *Symbolism*, 34; idem, *Process and Reality*, 83-9.

Chapter Four

Bateson's Theory of Double-Binding and Meta-Context

By discussing Russell's Theory of Logical Types in *Principia Mathematica* (1910-3), Gregory Bateson shows why paradox emerges and how opposite categories in a paradoxical situation can be interrelated and advanced to a higher type of context. The central thesis of Russell's Theory of Logical Types is that "there is a discontinuity between a class and its members. The class cannot be a member of itself nor can one of the members be the class, since the term used for the class is of a different level of abstraction—different Logical Type—from terms used for members."[1] In other words, the class is the type abstracted from its members while the members are the types that refer to concrete things. In this sense, "the name is not the thing named but is of different logical type, higher than that of the thing named."[2] The name is to the thing named as the class is to the members. The name itself is "of a different level of abstraction" from the thing or the object named.

The development of logical types is concretely shown in communication and play. In this regard, Bateson points to the fact that "the word cat cannot scratch us."[3] The word cat is the type of class. It is a name distinguished from the real animal we call "cat." Bateson writes, "A message does not consist of those objects which it denotes."[4] He observed the following:

> What I encountered at the zoo was a phenomenon well known to everybody: I saw two young monkeys playing, i.e., engaged in an interactive sequence of which the unit actions or signals were similar to but not the same as those of combat. It was evident, even to the human observer, that the sequence as a whole was not combat, and evident to the human observer that to the participant monkeys this was 'not combat.'[5]

For Bateson, the signals of the monkeys are different from combat but denote combat, though not combat itself. The signals are the message or class form of combat. "This phenomenon, play, could only occur it the participant organisms were capable of some degree of metacommunication, i.e., of exchanging signals which would carry the message 'this is play.'"[6] This action does not denote "what this action for which it stands would denote."[7] In this play, the signals of the monkeys denote combat but do not denote combat itself. The play of the monkeys is the metacommunication of combat itself. In other words, the play does not consist of combat itself, it is the message expressing combat.

According to Bateson, however, these logical types of communication are not developed simply by the distinction of the message from its objects. The logical types do not always follow Russell's ideal, which distinguishes the class from the members, that is, the message from the objects. Russell indicates that a paradox occurs when the class contains itself as a member. A paradox is caused by the non-distinction between the class and members or the message and the objects.[8] Thus Russell understands that the paradox can be eliminated in the distinction between them. Bateson shows, however, that "paradox is doubly present in the signals which are exchanged within the context of play, threat, etc."[9] When the play does not denote what its action would denote, it contains a paradoxical situation of not-denote and denote. Of course, not-denote and denote have different logical types. The former is higher than the latter in the logical types. Yet, Bateson argues that the distinction between the logical types is not always kept well in the complex process of communication. He notices the fact that there exists "histrionic play, bluff, playful threat, teasing play in response to threat, histrionic threat."[10] These phenomena show that a logical type is intermingled with another type. While real life is a context, play is the context of the context (i.e., metacontext). Yet play does not stop at play itself; its effect is linked to the real life situation. The context is not clearly distinct from the metacontext in the mixture of logical types. For example, "in the Andaman Islands, peace is concluded after each side has been given ceremonial freedom to strike the other," but "the ritual blows of peace-making" are often mistaken "for the real blows of combat."[11] The frame "This is play" or "This is ritual" is dissolved in this event. The peace-making ritual is changed to a battle.

This complexity of the logical types is observed in the phenomenon of the schizophrenic in more detail. Bateson claims that the schizophrenic has trouble in dealing with the distinction between the context and the metacontext. The schizophrenic finds it difficult to link the messages that he utters or gains in relationship with other people to the objects to which the messages refer. The communicational mode is the way of properly relating the messages to the objects in their distinction.[12] The difficulty of the schizophrenic is the confusion of the logical types between the messages and the objects. "He [the schizophrenic] has special difficulty in handling signals of that class whose members assign logical types to other signals."[13] The class and its members are distinguishable but not separable. In the confusion of the logical types, the message (i.e., the class) and the objects (the members) are intermingled or separated. In the disorder of the message and its object, either the message is unrelated to the context of its objects or the context of the message cannot be formed in confusion with its objects. Bateson writes, "[s]he omits what would be put on the procedural parts of the telegraph and modifies the text of his message to distort or omit any indication of these metacommunicative elements in the total normal message."[14] In this way a metaphoric statement is not labeled about context; there is no relation between the context and its metacontext.

Bateson also notices the fact that "schizophrenic commonly avoid the first and second person pronouns."[15] This phenomenon shows that they are reluctant to elucidate what kind of messages they express. They make a message obscure by avoiding concrete referents such as the first and second person pronouns delimiting the dialogical context of the message.

According to Bateson, "certain symptoms of human pathology called schizophrenia are, in fact, the outcome of maltreatments of logical typing."[16] The class is not clearly distinguished from its members in the vague distinction of logical types. Double binding results from the non-discrimination of different logical types; the wider context is considered within the narrow context.

> There may be incongruence or conflict between context and metacontext. A context of Pavlovian learning may, for example, be set within a metacontext which would punish learning of this kind, perhaps by insisting upon insight. The organism is then faced with the dilemma either of being wrong in the primary context of or being right for the wrong reasons or in a wrong way. This is so-called double bind.[17]

Two different contexts are intermingled so that one has difficulty in understanding what the problem is and what its solution is. Since each method is different in each context (i.e., a right method in one context can be wrong in another), a method can be right in wrongs ways or be wrong in right ways in "conflict between context and metacontext."

Bateson points out that the environment of hospitals for both personnel and the patient often brings a double binding situation. Though hospitals exist for the patient, the system intended for personnel brings inconsistency or conflict between them.[18] In this situation of double binding, since the therapist and the patient do not have trust in each other, the patient is uncomfortable both when the therapist does good and when (s)he does not do good. The benefits of personnel and patient are related to different contexts, but these contexts are not always clearly distinct in reality.

This double bind situation is not limited only to the schizophrenic. "The double bind also occurs in normal relationships. When a person is caught in a double bind situation, s/he responds defensively in a manner similar to the schizophrenic."[19] When an individual cannot explain contradictory messages, s/he takes "a metaphorical statement literally."[20] For instance, "one day an employee went home during office hours. A fellow employee called him at his home, and said lightly, "how did you get there? The employee replied, "by automobile."[21] This situation describes confusion between two different contexts in communication. While the caller asks metaphorically, the receiver responds literally in a contradictory situation in which he is at home during the time he should be in the office.

Of course, the mixture of metaphor and reality in a paradoxical situation shows the complex phenomena of human mind and communication in the transformation of logical types. In aesthetic enjoyment and religious rituals, the class and members are often intermingled with each other; human beings have developed their sensation and consciousness in the complexity of logical typing. Metacontext and context are entangled in the more complex form of communication in which paradox is implicitly present with conflicts and incongruence between two different contexts.

In sum, Russell's distinction between the class and members is the attempt to build mathematics upon logic without contradiction. However, such a distinction is not easily made in the world of facts. Many facts form complex phenomena that would not easily follow the distinction between the class and the embers as in Russell's solution of paradoxes. The facts, Bateson observes, show not only the different logical types of contexts but also paradoxes and double binds shaped in the conflicts between the context and its metacontext; and these features have complex structures that cannot be simply solved in the class-member distinction at the level of abstraction as in mathematics.

FACT-VALUE DISTINCTION IN BATESON

According to Bateson, double binds or paradoxes observed in the facts show the discontinuity of logical types or patterns in the conflict between context and metacontext. Therefore, double binds imply the loss of balance in discontinuity. A variety of logical types exist in the facts, but Bateson notices that such logical types are intricately entangled in their discontinuity, which causes double binds.

On the other hand, for Bateson, value exists in the enhancement of patterns between context and metacontext. On the other hand, value exists in the enhancement of patterns between context and metacontext. One enjoys his/her value in the intensity of pattern in the great chains of connections. Bateson does not attempt to eliminate double binds or paradoxes by distinguishing context from metacontext. Rather, he intends to heighten the type of double binds in the intensity of patterns, which would extend the horizon of contexts. In other words, a double bind can be dissolved by introducing another double bind. However, the latter type of double bind is one step higher than the former, and in this process the pattern between context and metacontext enhances the intensity of connection and elevates the logical type.

In this intensity of patterns, Bateson's notion of value is based on the relationship of organisms. An organism is not independent but a relational reality whose value is neither only in increasing nor only in decreasing. According to Bateson, value is the realization of harmony or balance between organisms in the correlation of their patterns. "For all objects and experiences, there is a quantity that has optimum value. Above that quantity, the variable becomes toxic. To fall below that value is to be deprived."[22] In this sense, value is not the monotonous value in isolation from the environment in which the organism lives. For Bateson, value is a derivative not of the subjective sense but of relations and patterns between organisms, its value is optimized in relation to others.

In this context, Bateson emphasizes the patterns connecting all living beings. On the basis of human-human and human-nature relations, Bateson understands value in terms of patterns, which continuously link the different logical types of organisms.

That we observe the shape, relation, and context of an organism is to regard the organism as a living being in a larger whole. Bateson calls this task of connection metapattern, i.e., a pattern of patterns.[23] The process of a metapattern is the process of connecting the different logical types, thereby extending the horizon of contexts. The first-order connection has a different logical type from the second-order, and the second order is different from the third-order. This connecting pattern shows the intensity of the relationship between organisms. Crabs, lobsters, horses, and human beings have different logical types, but are interrelated in the metapattern.[24] Bateson understands organisms as relational beings in a pattern of patterns. One organism is understood only in relationship to others. Each organism has its own logical type, whose balance is in conjunction with other types.

Bateson develops his notion of value by analyzing the characteristics of Balinese culture. To show no cumulative interaction in Balinese culture, Balinese notes that "the lack of climax is characteristic for Balinese music, drama, and other art forms. . . . Balinese music does not have the sort of rising intensity and climax structure characteristic of modern Occidental music, but rather formal progression."[25] Cumulative interaction is the linear structure in forming value. This cumulative interaction draws the curve of value reaching a climax and then falling, which strengthens the case for "schismogenesis." Schimogenesis is formed in pursuing an increasing or decreasing monotone value. Bateson writes, however, "Schismogenic sequences were not found in Bali."[26] The Balinese social system motivates the people toward the endurance of the steady state by precluding the maximization of simple variables and placing the value system in balance.

Because the people put their values in social relationship rather than in competition, they do not pursue their ideal in separation from the social system. The people and villages are never involved in maximizing simple variables. Certain positive values in balance are always emphasized in Bali. In this value system, "the driving force for cultural activity is not either acquisitiveness or crude physiological need."[27] The people are not interested in accumulating wealth and thus can enjoy food sufficiently every moment. They find the meaning and importance in artistic and ritual activity where much food and wealth are lavishly used. For the Balinese, the communal system places individual values in a chain that prevents schismogenic sequence. The logical type of the community is more complex and higher than that of individuals in the connection of patterns. This structure is determined by the intensity of patterns and contexts in which each individual is closely bonded.

From Bateson's perspective, the pattern "motivated in terms of a single linear scale of value"[28] does not match the value scale of organisms, which is not simple and monotone but complex in multidimensional context. In this scope, Bateson finds the value not in the thing-in-itself but in the relationship between various factors in contexts. Value is not intrinsic to the object itself. Value is shaped in the process of complexity, which continuously connects different contexts. From Bateson's perspective, the Newtonian world based on absolute reality view and reductionism developed by the subject-object dichotomy cannot describe the message of communication. According to Bateson, a message is not the simple object but always dependent on the context, which can be modified in relationship with another context. Contexts and the context of contexts are real and functions to modify messages. The value of messages exists in this connection of contexts. Value is not reduced to the object itself but realized in the correlation of contexts. For Bateson, a thing-in-itself has no meaning and value without its context. "Nothing will come of nothing."[29] According to Bateson, context is a "pattern through time."[30] When we say a being exists, the being must have "story." To have a story means to have information about the environment and context from which a being comes into existence. Words and actions are meaningless without context.

In a similar fashion, value is not reducible to the subjective. From Bateson's perspective, the empiricism or subjective idealism articulated by John Locke, Berkeley, and David Hume understand value as a private event based on sense-perception; value is only a derivative of the subjective sense and is only explained as a dimension of desire. In this context value is defined in terms of subjective sense-perception.[31] According to Bateson, the item felt and enjoyed in experience is regarded as a derivative from sense or, further, as a purely subjective tentative. In this paradigm it is impossible to regard experiences as the constructive element of the contexts. All experiences are formed by subjective sense perception and impression. Yet, Bateson regards the experience of organism as information of the really existing context. The context is the context including an experiencing subject as part of the relation between organisms. Value is not a product of secondary impressions emerging in the mind based on the sense-perception. Sense-perception and impressions are deeply rooted in the context. They are not independent of other elements constructing their contexts, and value is formed in the pattern that connects all living things through contexts of contexts. In this structure "a mind is an aggregate of interacting parts or components."[32] Impressions in a mind are constituted not only by subjective sense perception or reflection, but by the relationship of mind with its environmental conditions, including bodily feeling. In this system of mind, even single subatomic particles take part in the interacting parts of the mind. "The explanation of mental phenomena must always reside in the organization and interaction of multiple parts."[33] Value is achieved by satisfying this condition of mind. This mind operates not in simple subjectivity but in the complex structure of patterns connecting all living organisms. With the pattern of connecting the facts shown in each context, value lies in the evolutionary process of the organism that modifies its context and logical types.

THE CONNECTION OF DIFFERENCES

The interconnection between the two different contexts faces a vagueness of meanings entailed by the parallel between the conceptual images. David Hall maintains that

> if we try to stipulate in too refined a manner, we risk the creation of alternative semantic contexts which are not productively related one to the other. The standard way of saying this is to claim that if language $S1$ relativizes concepts $t1...n$ and language $S2$ relativizes concepts $r1...n$, then the immediately

> preceding English sentence entails the consequence that (assuming *S1* is the English language) *S1* relativizes both *t* 1...n and *r*1...n. Thus, the intent of the English sentence, *"Knowledge" and the Chinese word, zih, have quite distinctive conceptual contents* is compromised by the fact that the norms of the English language determine the meanings of the sentence, including of course, the English meaning of the Chinese word, *zih*.[34]

For instance, a semantic complexity is well shown in the situation in which the Chinese word "*zih*," which contains the meaning of "awakening" the principle of mind and nature through self-cultivation and the investigation of things, is translated as "knowledge" in English. In a stipulated manner, the meaning of knowledge continuously entails alternative semantic situations for matching a word from another cultural context.

Hall presents the vagueness of semantic contexts by comparing two different contexts. For the pattern connecting different contexts, Hall's citing of Bateson's connective method is noticeable in relation to "intertheoretical vagueness."

> Intertheoretical vagueness is a type of semantic vagueness occasioned by the refusal or inability to employ a term in a single stipulated sense. Gregory Bateson discusses intertheoretical vagueness under the rubric of 'Learning III,' which involves an awareness of the context of theoretical contexts leading to an experience of the parity of theories.[35]

Bateson's Learning III refers to the process of developing and extending one's own context in connection with other contexts. Bateson's method of connecting different contexts is based on the concept of "difference." "The effects of difference are to be regarded as transforms (i.e., coded versions) of events which preceded them."[36] Difference is the nature of relationship and presumes the interaction of two. For example, when we assume that X is the information of a context and Y is that of the other context, XY becomes the aggregate of the information class that both contexts attain. XY is the meta-context (i.e., the context of context) in terms of each X and Y. In other words, the relationship of the two comes from difference while the effects of difference transform the relationship into a higher level by providing new information.

Bateson's argument of a meta-pattern connecting different contexts relies on the difference-in-relationship rather than on matching the contents or conceptual images derived from each context. This difference often entails conceptual vagueness in applying one context to the other. Yet, the failure to notice such difference in a stipulative manner incurs the distortion of the meanings and contents of words rooted in each cultural and historical tradition.

"Intertheoretical vagueness" noted by Bateson and Hall should be understood in this context. That is to say, in semantic vagueness (or paradoxes) appearing in the shift from one context to another context (metacontext), a comparative method between the two is instigated by the connective pattern between different types, whereby semantic contexts are not fixed in meanings but open to a wider context. Therefore, the vagueness of meanings formed in connecting different theories furthers to instigate their relationship. Their vagueness should not be reduced to a certain sense at the cost of too much clarity.

NOTES

1. Gregory Bateson, *Steps to An Ecology of Mind* (New York: Chandler Publishing Company, 1972), 202.
2. Gregory Bateson, *Mind and Nature* (New York: E.D. Dutton, 1979), 229.
3. Bateson, *Steps to An Ecology of Mind*, 180.
4. Ibid., 181.
5. Ibid., 179.
6. Ibid.
7. Ibid., 180.
8. Ibid.
9. Ibid., 182.
10. Ibid., 183-4.
11. Ibid., 182.
12. Ibid., 205.
13. Ibid.
14. Ibid., 236.
15. Ibid., 235.
16. Bateson, *Mind and Nature*, 125.
17. Bateson, *Steps to An Ecology of Mind*, 245.
18. Ibid., 225.
19. Ibid., 209.
20. Ibid., 209.
21. Ibid.
22. Bateson, *Mind and Nature*, 54
23. Ibid.
24. Ibid., 11.
25. Bateson, *Steps to An Ecology of Mind*, 113
26. Ibid., 112.
27. Ibid., 116.
28. Ibid., 121-5.
29. Bateson, *Mind and Nature*, 45.
30. Ibid., 14.

31. Bateson, *Steps to An Ecology of Mind*, 251.
32. Bateson, *Mind and Nature*, 92.
33. Ibid., 93.
34. Hall, "On the Academics of Deception," in *Self and Deception*, 254.
35. Ibid., 251.
36. Bateson, *Mind and Nature*, 92.

Chapter Five

Non-directed Order and Harmony

This chapter discusses the issue of paradoxical combination developed by *Yijing* (the Book of Changes), one of the primary classics in the Chinese traditions. By critically evaluating the theory of change manifested in *Yijing*, I introduce a new paradigm for *Yijing* with the theme of non-directed order and harmony through Ilbu Kim's Jeongyeokdo and Jaewoo Choi's Donghak movement.

Yijing, regarded as a product of Fu Xi (ca., 4700 BCE),[1] King Wen (1232-1135 B.C.E.), and Wen's son the Duke Dan (ca., died 1094 B.C.E.) of the Zhou dynasty (1150-249 B.C.E.), has been known with its additional texts and ten commentaries attributed to Confucius (551-478 B.C.E.) under the name of "Ten Wings."[2] The core subject in these texts and commentaries of *Yijing*, composed of sixty-four hexagrams,[3] is the interaction of heaven, earth, and human being, so that the cosmological motif becomes the dynamic tension and transformation of all myriad things constituting the world, or the change and transformation of things in time. *Yijing* attempts to explain the realm of the unconscious or the spiritual as what cannot be reached by human reason. From the perspective of *Yijing*, the internal mind and the external world of things are unified through intuition. This view is agreeable with Jung's argument of meaningful coincidence between the psyche and the physical event in synchronistic phenomena.

In *Yijing* all things are defined by way of organic interrelationship, in which the reality of life shows the process of change. According to Hellmut Wilhelm,

> It is only abstract thinking that takes them out of their dynamic continuity and isolates them as static units. If we seek the parallel to this aspect of change among the concepts of our Western thought, it might be the application of the

category of time to phenomena. Within this category everything is indeed in a state of transformation. In each moment the future becomes present and the present past.[4]

The principle of change does not refer to simple change but to the change in the process of transformation, in which all beings are situated. The foundational principle of transformative change is developed not in the abstractedness of concept and essence of being but in concrete phenomena understood in immediate experience as irreducible to the dualistic form of either A or not A. Since *Yijing* concerns itself with process, its logical pattern is distinguished from abstract logic or formal logic in which truth and falsehood are clearly divided. It is beyond the demarcation between truth and falsehood that a correlation of antithetical elements is creatively developed in a paradoxical system.

The paradoxical relation of *Yijing* has shown the character of the thinking system of the East Asian tradition, which has noticed opposite situations in complementary relation. With regard to the issue of paradox, Sang Yil Kim articulates the distinction between the West and the East with Aristotle's logic and the issue of Bertrand Russell's liar paradox presenting the problem of ascribing the value of truth to a liar's statement "I am lying." This problem raised by Russell shows that, if that sentence is true, it becomes false, while if that sentence is false, it becomes true because the speaker making that statement is a liar. According to Sang Yil Kim,

> In Aristotle's logic, the Law of Contrast and the Law of Excluded Middle deal with the problem of the true and false in the dualistic way. It is the Law of Contrast that 'the true is true but not false' and the Law of Excluded Middle that a proposition should be true or false. However, the Liar paradox manifests the logic that the true is the false and vice versa. . . . This Liar paradox is the well known logic in the East tradition. The western scholars using this type of logic such as Heraclitus, Meister Eckhart, and the mathematician Cantor have been regarded as having the heterodoxical perspectives excluded from the prevalent western tradition. . . . [That is to say] Eckhart's statement that the human being is God or Cantor's proposition that the infinite number is the very finitude was regarded as heretical views in those days. In a word, the traditional and orthodox logic in the East was the heterodox logic in the West that was easily neglected as a minor point of view.[5]

While the Western tradition has regarded the paradox as something pathological, the Eastern tradition has regarded it as the basic method and starting point for creative process. Under Aristotle's logic pursuing rationality at the cost of eliminating the paradoxical such as "fuzzy" or "chaos," a proposition cannot be both true and false but should be either true or false. However, true and false are both aspects of a thing in *Yijing*. The opposite elements of you and me, my mind and nature, God and the world, or Heaven and Earth are not independent realities but the complementary characters of yin and yang formed in an organic relation. They are not static in the dualistic way of true and false but always changed and transformed by the continuous cycle of true and false.

From the instance of the liar paradox, Kim examines the language of paradox in *Yijing* with regard to the problem of paradox in the set theory raised by *Principia Matematica* (1910-3) written by Whitehead and Russell. The problem of paradox usually called "Russell's Paradox" occurs in the intermixture of the class type of language and member type of language, that is, the confusion of "meta language" and "object language."[6] In other words, the paradox occurs when "class (meta language) contains itself as elements (i.e., members, object language)."[7] That is to say, in the sentence of Russell's Paradox, "when a liar told a lie, the speaker's statement becomes true because the speaker is a liar," the language referring to the situation of "when a liar told a lie" is the object language or the member type of language. On the other hand, the language indicating the situation of "the speaker's statement becomes true because the speaker is a liar" is the meta-language, that is, the class type of language.[8] Thus, when the class is confused with the member, that is, when the meta-language is confused with the object language, a paradoxical situation emerges.

This situation is clearly shown in another example of the "Barber's Paradox." In a rule that the barber shaves only those who do not shave themselves, if we include the barber himself in that rule, a paradox appears. In other words, if the barber does not shave himself, he should shave himself according to that rule, if he shaves, he should not shave himself. While the if-clause with a focus on the shaving activity is the object language, the main-clause referring to the barber himself is the meta-language.[9] When the meta type of language and its object type are intermingled, opposite statements, that is, true and false, are cyclically revolved.

Russell, who raised the problem of Aristotle's logic by bringing up issues of paradox, also attempts to disentangle paradoxical situations in the circulation of true and false by distinguishing class from member, that is, meta language from object language in his theory of logical type.

Russell indicates that paradox appears by overlooking the hierarchical type of language, so that we can solve paradox with the distinction between logical types. In other words, type 1 is individual members, type 2 is the set of the members, and type 3 is the set of sets.[10] This solution of the paradox through the ascent of the type follows, according to Sang Yil Kim, the way of "hierarchical-consistent logic" in which the lower and upper level of types are always demarcated by the heightening of the logical types.¹¹ This solution is based on the distinction between class and members as different logical types. This means that the part is the part and the whole is the whole, whereby the two different types cannot be intermingled with each other.¹² Therefore, Russell is not far from Aristotle's logic in that he regards the paradoxical as still something problematic. To put it another way, by attempting to cease the continuous cycle of true and false with the solution of it through a hierarchical-consistent method, Russell returns to Aristotle's logic although pointing out the problematic point of Aristotle's method.

Although different from Russell's, Bateson's solutions of paradoxes—metapattern, metacontext, and metarelationship—are still based on the way of hierarchical-consistency. Bateson attempts to solve paradoxes, i.e., double binds by heightening logical types through the intensity of connection between a context and metacontext. This method actually shows the hierarchy of logical types. For example, providing one bind to solve another bind and pursuing the pattern of patterns are both attempts to overcome paradoxes by bringing a higher logical type, i.e., the class of class actions.

Sang Yil Kim indicates two important factors of "self-reference" and "self-annihilation" to understand a paradoxical situation. While it is self-reference that the barber shaves himself by applying himself to the very rule he made, it is self-annihilation that the class or meta (i.e., the barber himself) turns to member or object language by annihilating the status of the class.¹³ In the same manner, for the Liar Paradox, while self-reference means that the liar refers to himself as the liar by including the speaker himself (class or meta) in his or her statement (members or object language), self-annihilation means that the liar denies his or her statement by that self-reference. In other words, self-reference continuously entails self-annihilation, thereby resulting in one's denial of oneself. True becomes false and vice versa by self-reference and self-annihilation.

Kim does not regard this problem of paradox as a simple logical issue. How to handle the paradox reveals the distinction between the Western and the Eastern traditions in forming any realistic world views. The way of understanding paradox reflects the central issue of the history of philosophy in the East and the West. In particular, the problem of the one and the many or that of the whole and the part shows their different metaphysical views. Plato's Idea, the notion of God as the One in the Christian tradition, and Kant's noumena, which constitute the main streams of the Western philosophical and religious tradition, maintain the transcendence of the one beyond the many of the phenomenal world. That is to say, such transcendent reality is outside the paradoxical situation of self-reference and self-annihilation.

On the other hand, in the Eastern tradition, particularly in the East Asian tradition of Buddhism, Confucianism, and Daoism, the relation between the one and the many is developed in a paradoxical relation with the circulation of true and false. In this manner a reality view is based on the statement in which A is both A and not-A that takes a different path from Aristotle's Law of Identity and Contrast. The relation between principle (*li*) and material force in Neo-Confucianism, emptiness and fullness in Buddhism, Dao and phenomenal things shows that a proposition (e.g., nothingness) is both A (i.e., nothingness) and not-A (i.e., fullness) or neither A nor not-A.

In this manner, Kim presents the circular-inconsistent logic for developing the perspective of paradox shown in *Yijing*. In other words, the issue of truth in *Yijing* is not linear but circular, whereby the pattern of harmony and order is naturally formed in the ceaseless increase of the dynamic circle of true and false or yin and yang. This method is a very different approach to the issue of paradox from that of hierarchical-consistent logic. The circle of yin and yang shown in *Yijing* does not mean a simple but rather a creative circle in that novelty is produced by change and transformation in the repetitive increase of the circle.[14] In other words, the state of harmony or order is issued not by eliminating paradox but by drawing a certain circular pattern from paradoxical situations of yin and yang or true and false.

In this manner the logic of *Yijing* is developed by connecting all opposites. Yin and yang describes the two opposite characters of the Supreme Ultimate, which become basic elements in the constitution of the individual lines called *yao* for trigrams and hexagrams. Yin yao expressed by a divided line means "the soft and yielding, the submissive" whereas Yang yao expressed by a solid line means "the hard and strong, the assertive." In the process of change, the yin and yang lines are expanded by the connection of each other to describe concrete phenomena of nature in "Four Figuration of Double Lines," or "Four Images." The eight trigrams are, therefore, formed by adding yin or yang line to those double lines (see Figure 5.1).

The Four Images shows that everything has the two attributes of yin and yang in their balance. Yet, yin and yang cannot have the state of eternal balance because they are always in the movement of change and tension. In this way of change, the eight trigrams are insufficient to describe the concrete features of the world, each trigram doubles to make the hexagram.

According to the numerical system of the *Yijing*, one (the Supreme Ultimate) is divided into the two, and the two are divided into the four. In the same manner, the four are divided into the eight, and the eight are divided into the sixty four. We read the following in Explaining the Trigrams, "They [the holy sages] brought these three powers [heaven, human being, and earth]

Four Images

⚌ ⚎ ⚍ ⚏

Group Yang (each first line undivided):

☰ *Qian* (heaven 1), ☱ *Dui* (lake 2), ☲ *Li* (fire 3), ☳ *Zhen* (thunder 4)

Group Yin (each first line divided):

☴ *Sun* (wind 5), ☵ *Kan* (water 6), ☶ *Gen* (mountain 7), ☷ *Kun* (earth 8)

Figure 5.1.

together and doubled them; this is why the Changes forms its hexagrams out of six lines."[15]

The hexagram refers to the process of change other than the completed or closed system of changes. In this manner the trigrams or sixty-four hexagrams in *Yijing* system can become more expanded by the additional symbolic lines of yin or yang and intensified by the continuous contrasts of contrasts.

The most crucial condition for linguistic activity in the *Yijing* sense is communicative activity in which one word makes its meaning in organic relation to other words. This view of language does not support a fixed picture of language within which a proposition should be either true or false. A proposition is not the issue of true or false but forms meaning and value in the circle of true and false by drawing a pattern in communicative activity. According to Hall and Ames,

> Language is the bearer of tradition, and tradition, available through linguistic expression and ritualistic evocation, is the context of all linguistic behavior. The language user appeals to present praxis and to the repository of significances realized in the traditional past, and he does so in such a manner as to set up deferential relations between himself, his communications, and the authoritative models invoked.[16]

The linguistic activity characterized by "the language of deference" is the pivot of *Yijing* language with "mutual resonance" of words. Each word constituting sixty-four hexagrams has not an independent meaning but presents a symbolic meaning in its correlation with others in sequential contexts. That is to say, Hexagram 33, *Dun* (Withdrawl) is in mutual resonance with other hexagram words such as Hexagrams 32, *Heng* (Perseverance), 34 *Dazhuang*

Hexagram 33, *Dun* (Withdrawl ䷠)

Hexagram 32, *Heng* (Perseverance ䷟)

Hexagram 34 *Dazhuang* (Great Strength ䷡)

Hexagram 35 *Jin* (Advance ䷢)

Figure 5.2.

(Great Strength), and 35 *Jin* (Advance) (see Figure 5.2). Also, such words have no referential meaning apart from their particular contexts.

This linguistic pattern of *Yijing* shows the way of "correlative thinking" on the basis of which a self means the relational self. From the inseparable structure of language and thinking, a self is constituted by interdependent relation with other cosmic events by way of which opposite elements are paradoxically combined. This structure of self developed in *Yijing* is not confined in logical consistency. It is based on correlative thinking with a focus on concrete contexts formed in the empirical world. Relational self is the self constituting its character in difference, which is not regarded as exclusive but correlative with self-identity. As Ames argues,

> Correlative thinking" is basic to "the art of contextualizing," which constitutes a self. Yin and yang are familiar metaphors used in the classical tradition to express contrast and difference. . . . The nature of the opposition captured in this pairing expresses the mutuality, interdependence, diversity, and creative efficacy of the dynamic relationships that are deemed immanent in and valorize the world. The full range of difference in the world is deemed explicable through this pairing. Yin and yang are ad hoc explanatory categories that report on interactions among immediate concrete things of the world.[17]

The notion of change in *Yijing* is rooted in the concrete world in which the self dynamically moves with the correlation of the opposites. Therefore, the idea of change is not an abstract concept but is a contextual notion developed in an attempt to describe immediate things grasped in the phenomenal world. In this process, the pattern of change is rhythmically formed in yin-yang relation of concrete things of the empirical world.

In other words, logically inconsistent relations are gathered in correlative thinking and language that constitute the self and the world. The source for such correlation is in the interchangeableness of opposite things. The opposite is not the substantial opposite but the relational opposite that can be interchangeable with its different aspects in dynamic tension, thereby contextually defined in the correlative manner.

In this sense self is not clearly defined by the law of contrast. It is based on the "aesthetic complex" transforming logical inconsistency into creative moments. The transformation of self is achieved by appropriating logically inconsistent terms into the aesthetic context in which a self enjoys the experience of novelty. Even if two different terms are logically inconsistent, they can be transformed to the creative relation by the aesthetic enjoyment of the self. Thus, Hall argues,

> Terms characterized by recourse to a cluster indifferent to the question of logical coordination are, nonetheless, contextually defined. Such 'definitions' must result from aesthetic juxtapositions which highlight the tensions of contrasting and conflicting referential associations against the background of an aesthetically complex, if logically inconsistent, context. Our understanding of such terms would have to be closer to the experience of 'enjoyment' and 'appreciation' than to that of an act of grasping cognizable import. The only hope of accommodating the incoherences, incongruences, and inconsistences embedded in cluster concepts is that the self appropriating these notions must be of the same flexible form as the notions themselves. In this case, a mind becoming like that which it knows lead to a seriously ambiguted self.[18]

"Ambiguted self" means the self that cannot be reducible to our focal self by our conscious activity. It is not confined in a logical self based on scientific rationality in which self can be clearly defined. The correlative terms of the opposites in *Yijing* assumes the ambiguity of the self, which attunes logically inconsistent notions in "an aesthetically complex context." This motif of *Yijing* originates in the fact that the Chinese tradition locates the value ideal in realizing a harmonious world view. This view does not refer to an abstract value system but to the correlative system of the real concrete world. Harmony is not attained in a logical reductionism but in incorporating logical incongruousness through the process of change. In this sense the notion of change in *Yijing* entails the transformation of the self by encountering the different world that cannot be easily described in logical consistency and scientific rationality.

This transformation of the self makes possible the aesthetic view of the world that converts the paradoxical relation into a creative moment with self-enjoyment. This process of embodying the aesthetic self accommodates the fringe or background of the focal self. In other words, the focal self is only a partial aspect of the whole self. It is always surrounded by a wider context encompassing the periphery field of the self. Ames says,

> A focal self inheres in the natural world as its field, and where it shapes and is shaped by the field in which it resides. The dynamic structure and regularity of the focal self is immanental, inhering within it, and making it ever continuous with its context. As such, it is constitutive in its relationship to its world. The focal self is not in any sense discrete or independent, but is rather intrinsically related to and interdependent with its field.[19]

Ames's argument about the focal/field self as developed in the Chinese tradition becomes the key to understanding the principle of change and transformation in *Yijing* that cannot be explained within the frame of the focal self. Because the focal self grasps the flowing of things in a fixed picture, their real concrete feature within moving process is easily overlooked within the focal self. The important issue in this discussion of the self developed in *Yijing* is to understand the complexity of the ambiguous self with the field of the self formed in the aesthetic context. The creative transformation via the paradoxical combination of yin and yang, heaven and earth, retreat and progress cannot be limited only to the clarity of the focal self or logical self but entails the theme of the ambiguous self.

The ambiguity of the self does not mean the chaos of the self but the nonreductive way of the self, which is always open to change and transformation toward aesthetic harmony attuning different entities and terms in opposite relation. This character of the self starts with an emphasis on particular contexts. It proceeds to a different path from development with the first principle with the assumption of universality.

> The significant differences between the metaphysician Plato (to the extent that we want to continue this unfortunate caricature of a more complex philosopher) and the Chinese model are many, the most obvious being that the senses of order to which they subscribe—Plato beginning from first principles and classical Chinese thinkers from particular details—are irreconcilable.[20]

In other words, while Plato's metaphysics stipulates concrete and empirical contexts with the criterion of universal value or the Idea, the classical Chinese tradition defines the value of beings in particular details and contexts. This does not mean that the world-view of *Yijing* pursues only empiricism. This perspective of the Chinese tradition is different from the empiricism focusing on private events based on sense-perception. From this empiricist perspective, value is defined in terms of subjective sense-perception. In this empiricism the item felt and enjoyed in experience is regarded as a derivative from a purely subjective sense. In this manner of empiricism, it is impossible to regard experience as the constructive element of the context.

From the *Yijing* perspective, value is not a product of secondary impressions emerging in the mind based on sense-perception. Sense-perception and impressions are deeply rooted in context. They are not independent of other elements constructing their contexts, and the sense of order is formed in the pattern that connects all living things through contexts. Impressions in a mind are constituted not only by a subjective sense perception or reflection but by the relationship of mind with its environmental conditions. Value is achieved by satisfying this condition of mind. This mind operates not in simple subjectivity but in the complex structure of patterns connecting all living beings.

For the correlative cosmology of *Yijing*, all factors in the universe operate with their value system in balance and harmony with one another. The formation of a pattern in the empirical world and its endurance and transformation are required for the value-realization of things. A good pattern in the *Yijng* system includes the element that promotes the harmony and intensity of things by connecting all living worlds. In this sense value loses its meaning without any relation and reference to a particular context. With the pattern of connecting the particular facts shown in each context, value lies in the transformative process of things that modify their contexts.

The change and transformation of *Yijing* is in realizing harmonious relation between things. Such harmonious relation does not mean the simple addition of opposites but their paradoxical combination showing the basic logical system and the whole perspective of *Yijing*. The logic of *Yijing* is clearly distinguished from Aristotle's logic, which has been the basis of Western scientific logic and method. Whereas Aristotle's Law of Contrast (A and not A) refers to a logical fallacy, it constitutes the basic logic and central motif of *Yijing* that can describe the complicated and diverse contexts of self and the world.

Although the correlation of diverse elements is logically paradoxical, they are not ceased simply in chaotic situations but form a pattern of order in the process of change and transformation. Such relation is contextually rooted in the concrete empirical world, thereby promoting the self-encompassing of all the fringes of the self with the complementary pattern connecting the opposite elements. The self embodying the sense of order in the particular details practices its continuous change and transformation by maintaining the creative relation between the self and the world.

Group of yang

1 *Qian* ☰, 2 *Dui* ☱, 3 *Li* ☲, 4 *Zhen* ☳

Group of yin

5 *Sun* ☴, 6 *Kan* ☵, 7 *Gen* ☶, 8 *Kun* ☷

Figure 5.3.

ILBU KIM'S JEONGYEOKDO

Following the idea of *Yijing* by way of the connection between the opposites, Sang-Yil Kim develops the principle of change by bringing to his argument the theory of change of Ilbu Kim (1828-1889), one of the representatives of Korean *Yijing* thought:

If we see the circular diagram of Fu Xi's eight trigrams, we find the conversed direction between the group of yang and the group of yin (see Figure 5.3). But we can also see a certain directionality within each group. In other words, from number one to four, the arrangement of each trigram is directional and so does it from five to eight. The four trigrams in each group of yin and yang are directional. . . . However, Ilbu Kim attempts to advance the relation of the opposites by turning upside down even the direction in each group.[21]

In other words, Ilbu Kim's attempt was to shift the consecutive order of one to four in the yang group by arranging the relation between one and two (1→2) in consecutive order but that between three and four in reversed order (4→3). In the same way, for the group of yin, five and six are in consecutive order (5→6) but seven and eight are in reversed order (8→7).

Ilbu Kim's Eight Trigrams attempts to enhance the relation of the opposites by annihilating any directional order. It changes all directional consecutive order of the yang group (1234) and the yin group (5678) to the non-directional order of each yang (1423) and yin (5876). What Ilbu Kim attempts from this shift is to overcome the hierarchical order of all things by changing the order of the Supreme Ultimate, yin-yang, four images, and eight trigrams. This means that all individual lines in each hexagram are not subordinate to their higher levels of class. By articulating the non-directional relation, Ilbu Kim attempts to show that the part should not be reduced to the whole in some hierarchical order. Sang Yil Kim notes this point as follows:

In the hierarchical order, human is subordinate to God, nature to human, women to men, wherein reductionism and foundationalism of philosophy is formed. Any equality and autonomy cannot be expected in that hierarchy. Some directional order from *taiji* to hexagrams had been one of the reasons for the feudal system and gender inequality in the eastern society. . . . Ilbu Kim's trigrams attempted to make the world without any discrimination.[22]

Because the emphasis of Ilbu Kim's trigrams is laid on the circular system of natural phenomena in change and harmony, it cannot be viewed in a fixed system of directional order. Sang Yil Kim's perspective with his statement of Ilbu Kim's trigrams and argument for the unceasing connection of contrasting points shows that the principle of change in *Yijing* is unfinished but still in an on-going process. In this manner the trigrams or sixty-four hexagrams in *Yijing* system can become more expanded by the additional symbolic lines of yin or yang and intensified by the continuous contrasts of contrasts.

Sang Yil Kim points out that a certain directional order of *Yijing* had been one of the reasons for the feudal system and gender inequality in the Eastern society. However, Ilbu Kim's Jeongyeokdo symbolizes deconstructing all the hierarchical order between male and female, the ruler and the ruled, God and the world, destroying all discrimination of races, classes, and sexes.[23]

According to Sang Yil Kim, the comprehensive and transformational approach to order and disorder can be called "chaosmos,"[24] the compound noun of chaos and cosmos, which represents Ilbu Kim's Jeongyeokdo. The main purpose of Ilbu Kim's Jeongyeokdo is to show that there is no obstacle among nations, neighbors, and communities. It draws a new paradigm in which there is no conflict of ideologies.

This uniqueness of Ilbu Kim's Jeongyokdo opens a new horizon and new thinking system of *Yijing*. The birth, growth and maturity of the universe mean the cyclical movement of the supreme ultimate and non-ultimate. All the myriad things of the universe are in creative movement that circulates their differentiation and unification. The Supreme Ultimate is divided into yin and yang and thereby reaches the summit of differentiation. Then this process makes a turn to the movement of unification.

The purpose of *Yijing* is to make the perfect harmony of yin and yang. Sang Yil Kim applies those diagrams of *Yijing* to topological geometry. He argues that Ilbu Kim created his Jeongyeokdo in the 19th century in which period Euclid's Method had been challenged by Non-Euclidean way in the West. Whereas Euclidean geometries are 'directional and orientable' non-Euclidean geometries are 'non-directional' and 'non-orientable.'

Ilbu Kim's Jeongyeokdo corresponds to the non-Euclidean way and implies the four dimensional world by breaking a barrier between front and back, right and left, above and below, inside and outside. Those opposites support each other by making a perfect harmony. This is why Ilbu Kim calls his Jeongyeokdo "the World of Mirrors" in which things are reflected into one another by connecting the opposites.[25]

The World of Mirrors should be distinguished from the primitive society; the world breaking all the barriers of the opposites means not the world of non-differentiation without knowing the phase of the subject-object distinction but the world of "trans-differentiation." This world recognizes the stage of differentiation between the opposites (i.e., God/the world, heaven/earth, male/female, yin/yang) and constantly transforms their differentiation into a more mature and perfect harmony in a circular process.

Ilbu Kim's dialectical synthesis is de-centering a certain order and harmony, which both intensifies and extends the process of civilization. He deconstructs a certain directional and orientable point, i.e., the wholly other God, male-privileged society, human ego against nature. These examples are based on a directional, orientable, and hierarchical structure. The key of Jeongyeokdo is that each of them is central. Each trigram is not directed to a certain point but constantly connect the opposites, so that all hierarchical structure dissolves through the contrast of contrasts. Ilbu Kim's non-orientedness and non-directedness does not mean disorder or chaos but a new paradigm encompassing differences.

JAEWOO CHOI'S DONGHAK MOVEMENT

Donghak, which means the study of the East, is the representative model of Ilbu Kim's Jeongyeokdo to deconstruct any hierarchical system. Donghak, founded by Jae-Woo Choi (1824-64) in 1860, is also called *Chun-Do-gyo*. It was a revolutionary life-movement of the religious spirit of the Korean people in the 19th century, when the country was faced with a political, social and cultural crisis. The key of Donghak movement or *Chun-Do-Gyo* in Korean history was to destroy all hierarchical system of status, i.e., classism and sexism.

Chun-Do-Gyo articulates the nature of God in three modes: "*Shih Chun-ju* (waiting on or bearing God), "*Yang Chun-ju* (raising or fostering God)," and "*Che Chun-ju* (embodying God)."

To wait on God means to be filled with spiritual energy inside to feel the harmony of the spirit. *Chun-ju* means God while *Sh ih* means "writing on, bearing, serving." According to Yong Choon Kim, a Donghak thinker, "*Shih Chun-ju* means "man bears God" or 'man serves God.' *Shih Chun-ju* signifies that the human bears the essence of God within himself/herself, or the human serves God who is the Higher Spirit within the human mind."[26] *Shih Chun-ju* represents the organic relationship between God and the human spirit.

For God's interaction with the world, another important term in Donghak is *Yang Chun-ju* (raising God). Yang means "fostering," "developing," or "raising." That is to say, the world raises and fosters God.[27] In *Yang Chun-ju*, God is not unchangeable but movable, dynamically relating to the world. God is affected by and related to the world, just as the world is affected by and related to God. Raising God signifies that God does not control the whole process of the world. God does not only affect or condition the world but God is also affected or conditioned by the world in that God is raised and developed by the world.

If we commit evil, we come to hurt God bearing in ourselves. In other words, we have to develop and foster God in order for God to manifest Godself in our world. In this sense, God who is only in transcendent realm gives no meaning to our world. Yet, God's transcendence is necessarily required in that we have to transform our world by responding to and bringing God's transcendent vision. In this sense God's transcendence and immanence forms a dipolar pattern in a cyclical movement.

For another concept for God in Donghak, "*Che Chun-ju* (embodying God)" means to realize God in human body. Choi Shi-young writes, "we embody God by waiting on God and raising God. Every river, drainage, and lake is the blood and skeleton of the universe, the universe is the place where God dwells and embody Himself/Herself."[28] Thus God and the world are organically interrelated with each other. If the world suffers, God suffers. God and the world organically grow together and form a shared community.

The notion of God in the Donghak tradition is quite different from that of God as transcendent reality developed in the traditional Western theism in which God influences the world but not vice versa. In this theistic tradition, God is strictly distinguished from the world and thereby described as a controller. The world is totally dependent on God but not vice versa. God is described as almighty and immovable and dominates the world. This view of God has difficulty in explaining the problem of chaos and evil in the world. As a result, it was greatly challenged by an atheistic view with an emphasis on reason. Developments in science and reason signaled the end of the view of God formed in the Western medieval era and brought the beginning of the modern one. The beginnings of modernity are found in the new promises held out by science and reason. The cosmic view based most notably on the theocentric model of the universe and a central dogma was being overthrown. But instead, a new conception of human existence valued the individual and the individual's right to live his or her own life with an emphasis on reason and without intermediation of some external authority.

In the Donghak thoughts is found a different model of God from such a traditional Western theism, however. God does not the control the whole process of the world. God does not only affect the world but God also is affected by the world. The divine reality in Donghak is not a fixed or static being but always exists in dynamic relationship with the human mind and nature. In this sense, the divine represents the meaning of the ultimate in relation to the human nature. The divine signifies the force to bind heaven, earth, and human into peace and harmony.

Humankind always has been exposed to the world of mutual opposition-in- destruction. In the development of civilization, humankind has been overcome with industrialism and materialism. By focusing on material values, humankind has been losing moral values. This problem continues to destroy the relation among heaven, earth, and human beings. In terms of Donghak thoughts, the human being is not isolated but rather is interdependent with the rest of the world.

Mutual exclusion brings some negative results, according to Darwin's theory that only the fittest members of the species survive long enough to breed and pass on to future generations genes enabling them to survive as well. In this situation the unfit cannot adopt themselves to their environment and thereby will not survive. Mutual existence-in-support cannot be made under the theory of survival of the fittest.

In particular, human scientific achievement greatly affects our view of nature. According to the Newtonian-Cartesian scientific paradigm based on the subject-object separation, the object is passive whereas the subject is active. In this paradigm, nature is regarded as dead or barren, without any sense of the interaction with the human being.

This subject-object paradigm has contributed greatly to the Western scientific model based on the mechanical view in which the human being is separated from nature. In this mechanical paradigm, human as the subject is in opposition with nature as the object. The unlimited pursuit of industrialization and material wealth is taken at the sacrifice of nature.

From the Donghak perspective, the divine reality is not separated from the human mind and nature. The divine means the force of harmony and order for the world. The goodness of our mind and nature is based on the divine spirit, which is *in and with* all created entities in the universe. The truth refers to the state in which the divine permeates into everything constituting the universe; the harmonious state of the universe is based on the divine spirit and order to be actualized in the human world.

This relation between God and the world is rooted in the pattern of yin-yang dynamics. Yin and yang are defined in the relation of both opposition and fellowship. Both opposite images are not static but are of change and transformation in their fellowship. In this view, God does not control but always cooperates with the world, whereby God does not give any male image of active and controlling power, of independent reality without any receptiveness and responsiveness.

In yin-yang unity, God and the human world are not explained independently but in their complementary relation by way of which creative advance is motivated by the transformation of their relation. Yin and yang cannot be apart from each other, so it is the natural principle for yin and yang to be intertwined in a cycle in which God and humans influence each other, and the human history has been developed in relation to the divine.

In this manner, God cannot be defined without the human life context. God is the motivation for the creative change of human mind and the world, which should proceed continuously to harmonious relation by meeting opposites and by creatively transforming them.

NOTES

1. Fu Xi has been regarded as the first legendary sage king in Chinese history as mentioned in Commentary on the Appended Phrases of *Yijing*. See *Yijing*, Commentary on the Appended Phrases, 2:2.

2. The Ten Wings of *Yijing* are composed of Commentary on the Judgments (*Tuanzhuan* Wings 1 & 2), Commentary on the Images (*Xiangzhuan* Wings 2 & 4), Commentary on the Words of the Text (*Wenyan* Wing 5), Commentary on the Appended Phrases or Great Commentary (*Xici zhuan* or *Dazhuan* Wings 6 & 7), Explaining the Trigrams (*Shuogua* Wing 8), Providing the Sequence of the Hexagrams (*Xugua*, Wing 9), and the Hexagrams in Irregular Order (*Zagua*, Wing 10). The translation of the Ten Wings is based on *The Classic of Changes : A New Translation of the I Ching As Interpreted by Wang Bi*, trans. Richard John Lynn (New York: Columbia University Press, 1994).

3. Each line in the hexagram is constituted of yin (the broken line) and yang (the solid line), which symbolically refer to the dynamic change of things through the encounter of the opposites in the flowing of time. (see Figure 5.4)

4. Hellmut Wilhelm and Richard Wilhelm, *Understanding the I Ching [Yijing]: The Wilhelm Lectures of the Book of Changes* (Princeton, NJ: Princeton University Press, 1995), 26.

5. Sang Yil Kim, *Dong-hak gua Shin-Seo-hak* [The Eastern and New Western Study] (Seoul: Jishiksanupsa, 2000), 26.

yin: the broken line, --

yang: the solid line, —

Figure 5.4.

6. Sang Yil Kim, *Russell Yok-sol gua Guahak Hyuk-myung ui Gujo* [Russell's Paradox and the Structure of Scientific Revolution] (Seoul: Sol Publications, 1997), 25.

7. Ibid., 47. See also John L. Casti, *Complexification: Explaining a Paradoxical World through the Science of Surprise* (New York: HarperPerennial, 1995), 115-25.

8. Ibid., 25. See also Keith Simmons, *Universality and the Liar: An essay on truth and diagonal argument* (New York: Cambridge University Press, 1993), 1-19.

9. Ibid., 15-6. See also Bertrand Russell, *Introduction to Mathematical Philosophy* (London: George Allen and Unwin LTD, 1960), 181ff.

10. Alfred North Whitehead and Bertrand Russell, *Principia Mathematica*, vol. 2 (Cambridge, England: 1912), 317-40.

11. Sang Yil Kim, *Russell Yok-sol gua Guahak Hyuck-myung ui Gujo*, 61-68.

12. Whitehead and Russell, 404-34.

13. Kim, *Russell Yok-sol gua Guahak Hyuck-myung ui Gujo*, 47-53.

14. Hans G. Hertzberger, "Truth and Modality in Semantically Closed Languages," in *The Paradox of the Liar*, ed. Robert L. Martin (New Haven, NJ: Yale University Press, 1970), 25-45.

15. *Yijing, Explaining Trigrams*, ch. 2.

16. David L. Hall and Roger T. Ames, *Thinking Through Confucius* (Albany, NY: SUNY, 1987), 295.

17. Roger Ames, "The Classical Chinese Self and Hypocrisy," in *Self and Deception: a cross-cultural philosophical enquiry*, ed. Roger T. Ames and Wilmal Dissanayake (Albany, NY: SUYNY, 1996), 231.

18. David L. Hall, "Our Names are Legion for We are Many," in *Self and Deception*, 256.

19. Ames, "The Classical Chinese Self and Hypocrisy," 220-1.

20. Ibid., 200.

21. Sang Yil Kim, *Cho Gong-gan gua Hangook Munwha* [*Trans-Space and Korean Culture*] (Seoul: Gyohak Yungusa, 1999), 184-7.

22. Ibid., 186.

23. Sang Yil Kim, *Cho Gong-gan gua Hangook Munwha* [*Trans-Space and Korean Culture*], 186.

24. Sang Yil Kim, *Chaos and Civilization: The Crisis of Civilization and the Resurrection of Chaotic Goddesses* (Seoul: Donga Publication, 1994), 39.

25. Ibid., 432.

26. Young Choon Kim, "An Analysis of Early Chun-Do-Kyo thought" in *Korea Journal* 17, no 10 (Seoul: Koryo, 1977), 98.

27. Choi Dong Hee, *History of Korean Religious Thought*, vol. 3, Chun-Do-Kyo (Seoul: Munwhasa, 1978), 58.

28. *Canon of Chun-Do-Kyo* (Seoul: Chun-Do-Kyo General Assembly, 1970), 124.

Chapter Six

Wonhyo's Buddhist Thought of One Mind in the Organic Model

Ilbu Kim's Jeongyeokdo and Jae-Woo Choi's Donghak movements are in sequence with a Korean Buddhist monk, Wonhyo's wholistic vision of Buddhist doctrine, which is represented by his idea of the One Mind meaning the relational mind of all sentient beings. Wonhyo's notion of the One Mind serves the purpose to interconnect all separated minds. The One Mind as the source of all life indicates the indivisible state of mind, which is identified with the Buddha Mind based on great compassion and emancipation.

In this chapter I discuss Wonhyo's thought of One mind with the issue of paradox and correlative methods (called *Hwajaeng*) in the organic model. Wonhyo has been regarded as the most highly esteemed figure in the Korean Buddhist history. Among his works is included the commentary of the *Awakening of Faith in Mahayana* (or *Ta-Ch'eng ch'i-hsin lun*)[1] and Exposition of the *Book of Adamantine Absorption* (or *Vajrasamadhi-Sutra*),[2] which have been recognized as one of the finest works to convey the Buddhist doctrine of the Mahayana tradition. As Yoshito Hakeda says, Wonhyo's commentary is "among the standard commentaries on the *Awakening of Faith.*"[3] This evaluation is based on Wonhyo's wholistic vision harmonizing the opposite elements such as mind and nature, the subject and the object, principle and phenomena, or true and false in understanding the Buddha mind.

Wonhyo's idea of the One Mind is considered a cosmological explanation of existences in the universe. This realm of the One Mind is different from the soteriological ideal emphasizing the attainment of Buddhahood and the sacred world separated from the secular. Instead, Wonyhyo's explanation is about the peace and harmony of existences in this world through the dynamic interrelatedness between Buddha-mind and all other sentient beings' minds.[4]

Further, Wonhyo is concerned with how sentient beings harmoniously interrelate in society. Wonhyo's view of mutual non-obstruction of the One Mind is considered the cosmological harmony of all existences.

Wonhyo's perspective of the One Mind needs to be understood in relation to his living during a time when Korea was divided into three kingdoms—*Koguryo* (traditional dates 37 BCE. – 668 CE), *Baekje* (18 BCE – 660 CE), and *Silla* (traditional dates 57 BCE - 935 CE). Wonhyo's aim in exploring the One Mind is to find a way to overcome the conflicts among those dynasties. For Wonhyo, the purpose of Buddhism is to enlighten all sentient beings to be interfused into the One Mind. In this way the three diverged kingdoms can be harmonized and unified, whereby all disputes and conflicts can be overcome by a greater and broader horizon toward peace.

Wonhyo's main questions are how people's lives can be harmonized in equality; why the people born in Buddha nature are divided into different classes; and how harmony and order can be maintained in our lives.[5] With these questions, Wonhyo seeks a turning point to unification through the Great Compassion of Buddha mind, practicing unlimited love and mercy for the people suffering from the power game of three kingdoms. Such practice results from the mind of Mahayana (meaning the Great Vehicle), which is none other than the One Mind.

According to Wonhyo, no individual gains complete power or can exercise one's full power until one is given some environment. Specifically, one's power is exhibited only when an individual is in an organic unity and relates with other individuals. Where an individual is in a given in organic relationship with others, one is called to be powerful.[6] An individual exists interdependently with other individuals in organic society. Where an individual participates in organic unity with other individuals, it is said to be powerful and a wholistic existence. For the wholistic existence of each individual, the truth has neither direction nor fixation. The truth is dynamic and organic. The feature of the truth is described as the One Mind in which all contrasting elements are paradoxically combined.

Wonhyo analyze the human being on the basis of alaya-consciousness, or the storehouse consciousness operating in the depth of the human mind. This deepest realm of mind is called "alaya," which means the pure mind in which all discriminations are dissolved. He insists that Buddha and common people are not two different kinds but can be unified in the Storehouse Consciousness deeply embedded in the structure of One Mind.[7]

Wonhyo identifies the meaning of enlightenment with this mind of the non-obstruction, i.e., Dharma, the Way of Buddha. Here, the body of the truth is called the Dharma body, wherein one perceives the foundation of the world in the One Mind. Wonhyo's concept of Enlightenment is based on the foundational perception arising from alaya-consciousness.[8] Enlightenment and nonenlightenment are neither identical nor different in the One Mind. The two are identical in terms of the absolute reality in which all phenomenal distinctions are abolished. Yet, they are different in terms of the phenomenal distinction between arising (birth) and ceasing (death). According to the *Awakening of Faith*,

> Enlightenment and non-enlightenment have two types of characteristics. What two? The first is the characteristic of identity. The second is the characteristic of difference. As for the characteristic of identity, it is like assorted earthenware pots that are all of the same characteristic nature of clay particles. In this fashion the assorted karmic illusions of (manifestations) without outflows and ignorance are all the same characteristic nature of Thusness. . . . As for the characteristic of difference, it is like assorted earthenware pots that are individually all different. In this fashion, (wisdom) without outflows and ignorance are differentiated in accord with defiled illusions. (Similarly) the nature (of Thusness itself) and defiled illusions are (also) differentiated.[9]

In other words, enlightenment is not something to be made or attained; it is not the matter or form to be seen. The reason for the difference between enlightenment and nonenlightenment is that one is in the true reality while the other is in the phenomenal world. Wonhyo insists that the true realty refers to the One Mind. The original Enlightenment potentially exists in all people, yet they cannot see it in the phenomenal distinctions between the arising and ceasing of things. The original enlightenment, however, does not make any dualistic distinction. Such a distinction comes from our greed, ego, or the isolated self, which loses the connection with the alaya incorporating the self and the world.

From such a non-dualistic view, Buddha cannot be understood as a person or an object. Buddha is identified with Tathagata translated as Thusness or Suchness in which all distinctions—the subject/the object, the beginning/the end—are converged in a circular pattern. In the tradition of Mahayana Buddhism, the concept of Buddha is based on the dharma body, which makes possible the organic interaction of all sensitive beings. The dharma body is the ultimate principle based on the Enlightenment unfettered from discrimination and contradiction.

Wonhyo develops this thought more clearly developed in his commentary on the *Vajrasamadhi-Sutra*. According to the *Vajrasamadhi-Sutra*, "First is that practice that cleaves to phenomena. Second is the practice that cleaves to consciousness. Third is the practice that cleaves to thusness."[10] Robert Buswell translates Wonhyo's commentary on this statement as follows:

> The practice that cleaves to phenomena (while relying on the four noble truths and the twelvefold chain of conditioned generation) one cleaves to (the bodhipaksika-dharmas) in accordance with phenomena (that are governed by cause and effect). The practice that cleaves to consciousness: all sentient beings are merely products of the one mind. They cleave to the practice (of the four means of conversion [samgrahavastu]: giving [dana], kind words [priyavadya], helpfulness [arthacarya], and cooperation [samanarthata]) in accordance with (the principle that there is just) consciousness. The practice that cleaves to thusness: all dharmas are equal. One cleaves to the practice (of the six paramitas) in accordance with the thusness (that is equal). To 'cleave' here means to absorb these practices in the mind; it does not mean to cling to the subject-object distinction.[11]

While "thusness" is translated into "the Absolute," "samsara" is translated into "Phenomena," in which life and death (or arising and ceasing) are continuously circulated.[12] Wonhyo attempts to combine the Absolute with the phenomena on the basis of his theory of the One Mind. Then he illuminates the view of synthesis beyond antithetical aspects of teachings through the view of mutual non-obstruction between them.

Wonhyo's view of mutual non-obstruction of thusness and phenomenal things is considered a dynamic relatedness. Whereas the main axis of "the mind-as-thusness" is the principle, that of "the mind-as-samsara" is the phenomena. Thusness and samsara are distinguished at this point. All are interpenetrated without distinction in the mind-as-thusness while they make distinctions through the cycle of arising and ceasing in the mind-as-samsara.

Wonhyo points out the fact that the attribute of samsara is the particular or distinctive nature, whereas that of thusness is the universal principle or nondistinctive nature. These opposite factors seem to sharply contrast the two realms of minds. These two, however, are integrated in the One Mind. The Outline in The Awakening Faith is read as follows:

> Generally speaking, Mahayana is to be expounded from two points of view. One is the principle and the other is the significance. The principle is 'the Mind of the sentient being.' This Mind includes in itself all states of being of the phenomenal world and the transcendent world.[13]

Although the mind-as-thusness and the mind-as-samsara have their definitional difference in their predicates, they are integrated in the One Mind as the great vehicle. Therefore, Wal-lun Lai states Wonhyo's commentary as follows:

the One Mind may be pure in itself, but in its involvement with the world, it cannot help generating realities. When this Mind is not yet perfumed, it can still generate the good seeds according to the Dharma. When it is tainted but not so much as to lose its sublimity, the Mind becomes the indestructible spirit. However, further defiled, it produces karma and the surviving spark manifests itself only as the desire for bliss and the abhorrence of suffering. Finally, the Mind takes on mundane existence itself and becomes sentient beings.[14]

The mind of sentient beings is inclusive of the universal and the particular in the One Mind, which has both aspects of essence (or thusness) and function (samsara). According to The *Vajrasamadhi-Sutra*, "The minds of sentient beings are actually free from any discrete sense realms. Why is that? It is because the mind is originally pure, and the principle unsullied."[15] Wonhyo comments,

> 'The mind is originally pure, and the principle unsullied' represents original enlightenment. 'Soiled by the dust [of sensory objects, this world] comes to be called the three realms of existence' represents the common state of unenlightenment. 'If the mind is free from deception, there then will be no discrete sense realms:' this represents the stage of the actualized enlightenment, which takes one from unenlightenment back to original enlightenment.[16]

Buswell notes the following about Wonhyo's interpretation:

> Wonhyo explains that the one enlightenment is actually both the actualized and original enlightenments, which are nondual since "the perfection of the actualized enlightenment is in fact identical to the original enlightenment." Wonhyo then goes ahead to draw a tautology between the one enlightenment, the dharmakaya of the buddhas, and the original enlightenment that is inherent in all sentient beings. That immanent original enlightenment is the "enlightened inspiration that is innate in all sentient beings. . . , which influences the minds of sentient beings to perform the two kinds of action [benefiting oneself and others]."[17]

Every sentient being is potentially in the Buddha nature. The practitioner becomes immersed in one totality of Buddha nature through the practice of "benefiting oneself and others." This practice is to actualize the Buddha nature that inherently dwells in every sentient being, whereby the original enlightenment is united with the actualized enlightenment.

WONHYO'S *HWAJAENG* METHOD
AND PARADOXICAL COMBINATION

To practice the principle of Enlightenment and One Mind based on the non-dualistic way, Wonhyo develops his methodology called *Hwajaeng*, or

"Harmonization of All Disputes." According to Sung-bae Park, " Wonhyo's lifelong concern was to establish a foundation for T'ong Pulgyo, or Buddhism of Complete Interpenetration by means of *Hwajaeng*. . . . This is the essence of Wonhyo's thought, his central philosophy."[18] Wonhyo maintains that the true reality is beyond language. All discrimination covered by language is abolished in the true reality. Yet we human beings define things through language, and often mistake those defined languages for the true reality without considering the real character of things. In this way the true features of things are hidden by language.[19]

Wonhyo, however, emphasizes the fact that any definition or expression is made impossible without using language. Although we negate language, the negating way also has to depend on language. Here is the dilemma of language. Although the true reality is not totally revealed through language, we cannot express it without language. Language cannot only transmit the truth but also distort it. This is the dual character of language. The truth has both aspects that can be expressed and cannot be expressed.[20]

Yet, we have to express in language that which cannot be expressed. We cannot express anything without language, for any sign or symbolic system is another form of language. Wonhyo emphasizes that if we know the limitation of language and are free from being bound by that limitation, language can play an important role in helping us understand things. His theory of *Hwajaeng* starts from this view of language and attempts to overcome the two contrasting poles of affirmation and negation, true and false, or the thing-in-itself and the phenomenon.[21] Through the way of negation, Wonhyo avoids the attachment to the world. At the same time, however, he attempts to harmonize two extremes (attachment or detachment) through the negation of negation, which opens to the real feature of a single entity beyond any dualistic way.

Wonhyo's *Hwajaeng* takes, therefore, the epistemological shift to harmony and reconciliation beyond binary opposites and conflicts. By identifying the disintegration of the world with that of the mind, Wonhyo examines the possibility of the integration of the world through that of the mind. In this sense mind is not simply the subjective mind but the mind related with other minds. The true reality resides in the non-discriminatory character of the One Mind while the phenomenon represents the discriminatory character of the One Mind.

Wonhyo's Buddhist view proceeds toward the true reality per se in terms of non-discrimination in which the one is the many and the many is the one. In other words, the part is not the partial side of the whole but encompasses the whole itself. At the same time, the whole is not the synthesis of each part but encompasses the part in it. The One and Many are not substantial but relational, whereby all numbers are already in the number One. This paradigm does not support any dualistic distinction between the subject and the object.

The world in which the one becomes the many and the many becomes the one is regarded as the "Awakening State" in Buddhism. When all beings are awakened, they appear as the state of fullness, and their self-substances disappear in the fullness. In general, Buddhism calls the state of fullness "the emptiness." The emptiness is different from the western terms, "nothing," "nonbeing," and "vacuity" but similar to the opposite terms "fullness," "harmony," "interrelation." The ultimate purpose of Wonhyo's Buddhism is to fuse all realities of relational nature. Dharma-nature refers to a non-substantial and relational world.

Mahayana Buddhism had been developed by two mainstreams of thought: one is Madhyamika, or the doctrine of the Middle Path (the Theory of Negativity) represented by Nagarjuna (150-250) and the other is Yogacara, or the doctrine of Mere Ideation (Ideation Theory) represented by Asanga (410-500) and Vasubandhu (420-500). These two schools were sharply contrasted by their debate over the relation between form and emptiness.[22]

Wonhyo indicates the following about the reason for their contrast between the Schools of Madhyamika and Yogacara:

> The theory of Madhyamika negates all kinds of attachments and further negates all negated things, and thus it does not affirm the negating and negated agent. It is called the theory that is only 'sending out' but not 'pervasive.' On the other hand, Yogacara establishes all of the deep and superficial theories and deciphers the Way of Mind, so that it is called the theory of affirmation.[23]

From Wonhyo's perspective, the Madhyamika concentrates only on negating things while Yogacara only concentrates on affirming them. He argues that the Awakening of Faith in Mahayana presents the way to a combination of negation and affirmation. According to Whalen Wai-lun Lai,

> Wonhyo considers the AFM [Awakening of Faith in Mahayana] to be superior in understanding. The partial understanding of [those schools, Middle Path or Mind Only] are not yet the whole or totalistic understanding. The Buddha-nature is neither caused nor effected; it is truly ultimate yet truly mundane, simultaneously self and other, a transcendental entity which fully participates in samsara.[24]

According to the Awakening of Faith, the world of reality has two aspects, the absolute and the phenomenal. The aspect of the absolute is centered on principle while the phenomenal aspect is developed in a circle of birth (or arising) and death (or ceasing). For Wonhyo, each of these opposite natures in the One Mind also contains the opposite category in itself.[25] In other words, as the mind-as-thusness encompasses both the universal and the particular, so the mind-as-samsara does both of them. Given this, the statement that the two different kinds of Mind are incorporated into the One Mind does not mean that each of them takes either the principle or the phenomena of the One Mind. Thusness and samsara each contain the whole aspects of the One Mind.

In this sense, the Awakening of Faith states, "Each of these two aspects embraces all state of existence. Why? Because these two aspects are mutually inclusive."[26] Thusness cannot reveal the meaning of itself in words. Nevertheless, if we analyze the significance of thusness in words, it can be expressed as "empty" and "not-empty." "Thusness has two aspects if predicated in words. One is that it is truly empty (sunya) for [this aspect] can, in the final sense, reveal what is real. The other is that it is truly nonempty (a-sunya), for its essence itself is endowed with undefiled and excellent qualities."[27]

Wonhyo comments that these two aspects of the opposites are also applied to the mind-as-samsara, which embraces the one world of the principle and the phenomena. Here the empty describes the absolute in terms of principle while the not-empty describes the absolute in terms of phenomena.[28] In this manner the reason for describing the absolute in terms of both principle and phenomena is that the universal and the particular are interrelated with each other.

This way is based on the logic connecting the contrasting poles. While thusness (the universal) contains phenomena, samsara (the particular) contains principle. The logical pattern of Mahayana is distinguished from abstract logic or formal logic in which truth and falsehood are clearly divided. It is beyond the demarcation between truth and falsehood that a correlation of antithetical elements is creatively developed in a paradoxical system. For connecting thusness with samsara, Wonhyo comments, "Because these two kinds of Minds embrace the one world of the Reality, they are not separated from each other" by both containing principle and phenomena.[29]

A problem that Wonhyo identifies is the difficulty connecting each different predicate in thusness and samsara. While the predicate of the mind-as-thusness is "the interpenetration of impurity and purity," that of the mind-as-samsara is "the distinction of impurity and purity."[30] Wonhyo's method for dissolving such a difference is to add one predicate to the other subject. In other words, Wonhyo attempts to add the interpenetration of impurity and purity (the original character of the mind-as-thusness) into the character of the mind-as-samsara and simultaneously add the distinction of impurity and purity (the original character of the mind-as-samsara) into the character of the mind-as-thusness. According to Wonhyo, the Awakening of Faith implies adding their interpenetration into the mind-as-samsara.[31] This is observed in the explanation of "identity" and "nonidentity."

> Two relationship exist between the enlightened and nonenlightened states. They are "identity" and "nonidentity." (1) Identity: Just as pieces of various kinds of pottery are of the same nature in that they are made of clay, so the various magic-like manifestations (maya) of both enlgithenment (ansasrava: nondefilement) and nonenlightenment (avidya) are aspects of the same essence, Thusness.[32]

In other words, the identity between enlightenment and nonenligtenment indicates the same meaning as the interpenetration between purity and impurity while nonidentity is equal to the distinction between those two. The mind-as-thusness and the mind-as-samsara are interpenetrated by way of identity. The source of explaining identity and nonidentity in the mind-as-samsara is based on the interaction of enlightenment and nonenlightenment.

Awakening of Faith states the following in its Outline: "The phenomenal aspect of this Mind [the mind-as-samsara] indicates the essence, attributes (*lakshana*), and influences (*kriya*) of Mahayana itself."[33] Although samsara is identified with the aspect of the phenomena, samsara includes Mahayana itself. Wonhyo comments that the existence of Mahayana itself within the mind-as-samsara does not mean that thing-in-itself (Mahayana) follows samsara.[34] Mahayana itself is distinguishable but not separable from samsara. "The mind-as-samsara is grounded on the Tathagata-garbha (Storehouse Consciousness). What is called the Storehouse Consciousness is that in which 'neither birth nor death (nirvana)' diffuses harmoniously with 'birth and death (samsara),' and yet in which both are neither identical nor different." Wonhyo maintains, "displaying the Mahayana itself means the original enlightenment within the mind-as-samsara."[35] Identity and Nonidentity between enlightenment and nonenlightenment correspond to the logical pattern of 'neither birth nor death' and 'birth and death' or that of 'neither one nor two,' highlighted by the integrative method of the Storehouse Consciousness.

From this perspective, we can observe that the paradoxical combination between identity and nonidentity foster the deep interaction of the principle with the phenomena. According to Wonhyo, identity and nonidentity means that there exists the essence of Mahayana in the mind-as-thusness while there is Mahayana itself in the mind-as-samsara. In other words, Mahayana itself (samsara) can be tantamount to its essence (thusness), but both are not identical in the distinction between the essence of reality itself and the phenomenon of reality itself.

This paradoxical combination represents the nature of the Mind. Thusness is often used as the predicate of samsara and vice versa, whereby both are connected. Wonhyo states, "Thusness is equal to the original enlightenment of pure nature in the mind-as-samsara."[36] This does not mean that the two kinds of minds—the mind in terms of the absolute and the mind in terms of the phenomena—cannot even be distinguished. Although they are combined in One Mind, they have differences in their doctrinal meanings. Identity and nonidentity reveal this character of their distinction and unification.

In this paradoxical combination, Wonhyo explains the way developed from thusness to samsara and vice versa in the interaction of the principle with the phenomena. In other words, the actualization of the principle into the phenomenal world is made in that interaction. From this realization, the Storehouse consciousness and the original enlightenment do function properly in the phenomenal world. Through the working of the mind-as-thusness in samsara, the purity and impurity, the universal and the particular are unified in the One Mind. The principle naturally encompasses the phenomenal world and expands its meanings in relation to the other.

In the same manner the phenomena return to the principle in the One Mind, whereby the former also expands its meaning in relation to the latter. Although the phenomena or samsara means the secular developed in the circle of birth and death, it also actualizes the true reality in that circle through the practice of Buddha's Great Compassion and the harmonization of all disputes.

NOTES

1. The Awakening of Faith in Mahayana is said to have been written in Sanskrit by Asvaghosha. It was translated into Chinese in 550 by Parmartha, the Indian translator of Buddhist texts. This work has been regarded as a comprehensive summary of the essentials of Mahayana Buddhism and has greatly influenced the development of East Asian Buddhism.

2. Wonhyo is the central figure to interpret and analyze *Vajrasamadhi*. His commentary on the scripture is called *Kumkang sammaegyong-ron*. As Robert Buswell says, "Among Wonhyo's treatises, his Exposition of the Book o the Vajrasamadhi-sutra seemed to provide the most through and mature outline of his syncretic vision. . . . A study of his Exposition might also provide some valuable indications as to the role such 'apocryphal' sutras played in the development of uniquely East Asian forms of Buddhism." See, Robert Buswell, *The Formation of Ch'an Ideology in China and Korea* (Princeton, NJ: Princeton University Press, 1989), xiv.

3. *The Awakening of Faith*. translated with commentary by Yoshito S. Hakeda (New York: Columbia University Press, 1967), 9.

4. Sung Bae Park, *Buddhist Faith and Sudden Enlightenment* (Albany, NY: State University of New York, 1983), 37-42.

5. Youngseop Ko, "Wonhyo's Study of Unification," in *Wonhyo*, ed. Youngseop Ko (Seoul: Yemoon Seowon, 1993), 166.

6. Ibid., 191.

7. Wonhyo's commentaries of the Awakening of Faith are composed of Running Commentary (Commentary on the Awakening of Faith) and Expository Notes (Special Notes on the Awakening of Faith). In his Expository Notes, Wonhyo writes that Alaya refers to the One Mind in the wholeness of mind and body. Translation is mine. See Wonhyo, "Expository Notes on the Awakening of Faith," in *The Collected Works of Korean Buddhism*, vol. 1 (Seoul: Dongguk University Publication, 2002), 747.

8. Ibid., 747-8.

9. Quoted from *An English Translation of Fa-Tsang's Commentary on the Awakening of Faith*, trans. Dirck Vorenkamp (Lewiston, New York, 2004), 175-9.

10. Ibid., 234.

11. Ibid.

12. *The Awakening of Faith*. translated with commentary by Yoshito S. Hakeda, 32-6.

13. The Awakening of Faith, 28.

14. Whalen Wai-lun Lai, *The Awakening of Faith in Mahayana (T-ch'eng ch'i-hsin lun): A Study of the Unfolding of Sinitic Mahayana Motifs* (Ph.D. diss., Harvard University, 1975), 163.

15. Quoted from Robert Buswell, *The Formation of Ch'an Ideology in China and Korea*, 214.

16. Ibid.

17. Ibid., 206.

18. Sung-Bae Park, *Wonhyo's Commentaries on the Awakening of Faith in Mahayana* (Ph.D. diss., University of California, 1979), 73.

19. See Wonhyo, "Running Commentary on the Awakening of Faith," in *The Collected Works of the Korean Buddhism*, vol.1, 743-744.

20. Youngseop Ko, "Wonhyo's Study of Unification," in *Wonhyo* 184-5.

21. In his commentary on Vajrasamadhi, he argues that both agreement and disagreement are used for *Hwajaeng*. The two are in a complementary relation for one's own argument. Two opposites are paradoxically combined in Wonhyo's *Hwajaeng* method. See Wonhyo, "Commentary on *Vajrasamadhi*," in *The Collected Works of the Korean Buddhism*, vol. 1, 638.

22. Junjiro Takakusu, *The Essentials of Buddhist Philosophy*, ed. W.T. Chan and Charles A. Moore (Honolulu: University of Hawaii, 1947), 80-108.

23. Wonhyo, "Expository Notes," in *the Collected Works of Korean Buddhism*, vol. 1, 768.

24. Whalen Wai-lun Lai, 62.

25. Wonyo, "Running Commentary," in *the Collected Works of Korean Buddhism*, vol. 1, 753.

26. *The Awakening of Faith* 31.

27. Ibid., 34.

28. Wonhyo, "Running Commentary," 756-7.

29. Ibid., 743.

30. Ibid., 760.
31. Ibid.
32. *The Awakening of Faith*, 45-6.
33. Ibid., 28.
34. Wonhyo, "Running Commentary," 734.
35. Ibid., 735.
36. Ibid., 768.

Chapter Seven

The Theological Significance of Paradox in the Organic Model

A DIALOGUE BETWEEN CHRISTIANITY AND NATURE IN THE ORGANIC MODEL

In this part, I discuss McFague's ecological theology and explore the significance of nature in the Christian tradition. From a theological perspective, ecological concerns in the organic model can be addressed by applying the metaphysical principle of interrelatedness to our life-context. This application is developed by a practical principle of mutual existence to create a global community. The purpose of this principle concerns specifically how to practice a harmonious life in the modern chaotic world. In this part, I will discuss the ecological significance of the mind and nature in the organic model. I will argue that Christian thoughts are deeply connected with today's ecological issues and can help overcome the environmental crisis that our world currently faces. Religious thought has great value for the discussion of environmental issues. "As the human community struggles to formulate different attitudes toward nature and to articulate broader conception of ethics embracing species and ecosystems, religions may thus be a necessary, though only contributing, part of this multidisciplinary approach."[1] Given this necessity of religious thoughts in caring for nature, the Christian gospel can be reinterpreted in terms of its ecological aspects.

Materialism and selfishness have produced a mutual exclusion between God and the world, so that people's pursuit of material wealth in industrial societies conquers and suppresses the natural world. God and the world in the organic model are concerned about human needs in ecological care. Sallie McFague writes,

> God the sustainer is a further elaboration of how the creator and liberator God operates to insure planetary well-being. The sustenance—breath and food and all needful things—that creation must have to survive are provided daily and concretely by God. God the liberator will not only protect us against great evils and dangers—whatever would enslave and undermine us, but God the sustainer will also give us the most mundane, basic things we need to thrive.[2]

Stating that human need is more fundamental than human greed, McFague emphasizes that the earth we live in *is* the body of God. To recognize the earth as the body of God is based on our sense of mutual existence. The human ego and its desires may cause a break in the balance between God and the world and thereby lead to overexploitation of nature. Mutual existence represents the living principle of God-world harmony in which eternal peace is achieved without causing any harm to human beings or nature.

From this idea of mutual existence, McFague presents a new model for God-world interaction. This new model, McFague argues, is the "ecological economic" model. Emphasizing the "ecological economic" model, she argues that an individual is interconnected with others consciously or unconsciously. In other words, the concept of an individual cannot be defined without his or her community. The individual and community are not two independent entities. The essential nature of the individual is communal, whereby one is interdependent on the rest of the world. According to McFague,

> The relational model of self and world, built as it is on a flexible, fluid boundary of self and others, means that self-interest and altruism are not always opposed; in fact, they often converge. Just as one rejoices when a friend or a child gets a good job or an award (since one's own self is formed and nurtured by these relations), it is also imaginable that we would rejoice when a marshland is preserved for migrating birds or a pocket-park bill is passed in our city, if we believed that our interior landscape is formed by the exterior landscape. If self and world are not oppositional but connected, so that who we are is profoundly related to who the others are—including the others in the natural world—then well-being becomes a more common term; in fact, one's own well-being could not come about apart from the well-being of others.[3]

All lives exist in their interdependence on one another in their environments. They adapt themselves in their organic relation to natural environments. Therefore, ecology deals with all facets of lives in their interdependence. In other words, an individual life cannot be developed separate from its community. The ecological significance is found in the organic interaction of all elements of which the universe is made.

According to Cartesian dualism, nature is only the object separated from the human mind; it is the tool that can be dominated by the human being as a thinking subject. In this way, the Cartesian dualistic paradigm may be supportive of today's ecological crisis. Because the human being without natural resources cannot endure, he or she is defined in connection with nature. The human being is related organically with his or her environment. The mutual existence of lives and their dynamic relations take place in every group of life, (e.g. the interdependence of the tree root and bacteria or mold on each other). As McFague says, "the panda's unique digestive tract was designed with the help of bamboo shoots; human beings are also what we are because of where and how we evolved. . . . We are 'mixed up' with it in every way imaginable."[4] The landscape is covered by fallen trees and leaves, rotting organisms, and decomposed excrement. It is continually being broken down by water, sunlight, and microorganisms. All of these elements are placed in their organic relation to one another. However, the garbage produced by modern industrial society harms this organic relationship. This is why the ecosystem cannot accept contaminated materials. Their influences return to those who destroy the ecosystem. What goes around comes around. This ecological crisis also causes a crisis for humans by the killing of animals and plants for economic profit. By way of this, the ecosystem and human beings are interdependent on each other.

Theology should be deeply concerned with such an ecological crisis brought by human abuse of natural resources. The natural community is God's creative world, and human beings are responsible for preserving the earth. God's world is full of harmonious relationships between opposites with no discrimination of races or sexes. God's world is based on mutual existence between opposites. All opposite elements—heaven and earth, water and fire, mind and nature—support each other in mutual existence.

Jesus is the self-emptying God, who sacrifices himself for the world. Self-denial is one of the greatest mottoes in Jesus' message: "The first will be the last, and the last will be the first, meaning that the self-desire is the harmful result of which returns to themselves in the end."

Self-desire has been responsible for disintegrating the ecosystem by disregarding its ecological order. Human selfishness harms the natural environment by constantly exploiting natural resources, and the natural world returns its harm to the human world in a vicious circle. We are blinded by the accumulation of material wealth, while the world is faced with an ecological crisis including global warming. The accumulation of materials has meant that humans recklessly abuse the environment and its natural resources for their material wealth.

Peace for humankind will come about by realizing the infinite truth by embracing, respecting, and loving others. When human beings and nature respect and support each other, nature will continue to produce resources for the human world, while humans protect and love nature.

From the ecological viewpoint, the ultimate principle is the mutual existence to maintain peace and harmony of both human and natural worlds. The purpose of mutual existence is to benefit one another by practicing "self-giving" instead of the "self-interest" that prevails in the paradigm of mutual exclusion and opposition. In mutual exclusion, natural resources become depleted by human self-desire. The world has overlooked the fact that the earth is an organic life interdependent on human beings. Conquering the land and overusing limited natural resources, widespread industrialization and unlimited human selfishness has promoted the current ecological crisis.

The air pollution caused by the burning fuel by automobiles or factories is a threat to human life and the environment. It is one of the main causes of respiratory disease, bronchitis, and lung cancer. Lead and mercury in automobile exhaust may cause brain disease. Further, air pollution is responsible for acid rain, which harms agriculture, stunts the growth of trees, and corrodes stone architecture. It also acidifies water and weakens the productivity of land. Many trees and forests are being destroyed by acid rain.

Water is the source of life itself. The contamination of water is an enormous threat to the human community. Water contamination means that polluted materials are mixed with such waters as streams, lakes, rivers, or oceans. This environmental situation has put the ecosystem in such disorder that we may no longer be able to use the water resources in the near future. Wastewater discharged from factories and municipal sewers accelerates water contamination. It is also a threat to human health and thereby raises the rates of cancer and the birth defects.

A way to overcome this situation of environmental problems embodies the virtue of mutual existence in the incorporation of yin-yang creates the ideal environment for the rich resources of the natural worlds. Heaven and earth represent the natural worlds in the complementary relations between yin and yang. Heaven and earth in yin-yang unity produce the infinite foundation for the rich environment of nature without any suffering or insufficiency.

This yin-yang unity becomes the source of divine-human harmony. In this harmony, the human is divine, and the divine is human. In this divine-human harmony, human respect for nature is shaped naturally by the way in which human beings constantly transform themselves into a divine nature. This view represents the East Asian relational paradigm of correlative cosmology.

The seamless interconnection between the divine, human, and natural worlds that characterizes three traditions has been described as an anthropocosmic worldview. There is no emphasis on radical transcendence as there is in the Western traditions. Rather, there is a cosmology of a continuity of creation stressing the dynamic movements of nature.[5]

The divine-human-nature harmony is also based on mutual "existence-in-support." From the ecological perspective, the life of mutual existence refers to the feature of the true world.

The ecosystem is properly maintained by the unity of humans and nature. This means each element constituting the world is interdependent, whereby there is no obstacle between the human world and natural world. The laws for sustaining our planet are based on the relational paradigm of mutual respect: there are no natural disasters, no war, and no human greed, to disrupt the peaceful world. According to Peter Hodgson,

Our Western way of thinking is biased toward substances: substances, we assume, are primary realities, and events are the result of the interaction of substances. The ecological model reverses this priority: events are primary, and substantial objects are enduring patterns among changing events. Events are the complex interacting of entities, and the latter are simply relations. An entity is a mode of relating. This ecological insight bears striking similarities with Eastern, especially Buddhist, ways of thinking, and it offers a point of contract for inter-religious dialogue.[6]

This Ecological model deals with all facets of lives in their interdependence. Each individual life cannot be developed separate from its mutual community. In other words, each individual is interdependent on all others to be an individual. This ecological concern comes from the mutual existence of all elements of which the universe is made.

McFague presents the ecological model with the world as God's body. God's incarnation means that this world is identified with God's body. McFague writes that "if God is always incarnate, then Christians should attend to the model of the world as God's body. For Christians, God is not become human on a whim; rather, it is God's nature to be embodied, to be the One in whom we live and move and have our being."[7] God is both transcendent from and immanent within the world. From the Christian perspective, although this world is not identical with God's reality itself, it is the place where God's nature is embodied in our lives. According to McFague, "in our model, the body of God is the entire universe; it is all matter in its myriad, fantastic, ancient, and modern forms, from quarks to galaxies. More specifically, the body of God needing our attention is planet Earth, a tiny piece of divine embodiment that is our home and garden."⁸ Every breath we take depends on all the others in the entire universe, which is God's body.

Given this, the quality of relationship is the truth that we should practice to preserve God's body. The quality of relationship in the world as God's body is the God-human-nature harmony. McFague continues, "In order to care for this garden, we need to know about it; in order to help all creatures who constitute this body flourish, we need to understand how we humans fit into this body."⁹ The planet Earth in which we live *is* the divine embodiment. Rocks, trees, rivers, animals, and human beings are all intermingled in a dynamic chain. They all constitute the body of God, which is nurtured and advanced by their harmonious relationships.

From the ecological perspective, according to McFague, "everything is interrelated and interdependent." McFague argues that "'ecological unity' is both radically individualistic and radically relational. In an organism or body, the whole flourishes only when all the different parts function well; in fact, the 'whole' is nothing but each and every individual part doing its particular thing successfully."¹⁰ An individual is not isolated being. He or she is interdependent with other human beings and nature. This means that to live as an individual is to live as the individual involved in the world as God's body.

The self-centeredness completes the circle to self-destruction as a result of human greed. What goes around comes around. Human greed in self-centeredness causes the abuse of natural resources and also the problem of distributive injustice: the rich become richer and the poor become poorer. Yet, "human need is more basic than human greed." Human greed cannot take away human need. The world as God's body is the world realizing the distributive justice and sustaining nature. Human greed is a distorted form of human nature separate from God's way. In this sense, Jesus' message that "the first will be the last and the last will be the first" equals self-denial and self-emptiness in which human greed disappears and everyone benefits equally by meeting each other's needs and enjoying natural resources in a proper way. McFague continues to write the following:

> While there are many distinctive features of the Christian notion of embodiment, in an ecological age when the development of our sensibility concerning the vulnerability and destruction of nonhuman creatures and the natural environment is critical, we ought to focus on one: the inclusion of the neglected oppressed—the planet itself and its many different creatures, including outcast human ones. The distinctive characteristic of Christian embodiment is its focus on oppressed, vulnerable, suffering bodies, those who are in pain due to the indifference or greed of the more powerful. In an ecological age, this ought to include oppressed nonhuman animals and the earth itself.¹¹

The turning point of our consciousness from the center to the periphery is necessary to Christian embodiment; God's body should be the space where all the objects ignored by the ego-centeredness or human greed get attention in a recognition of their significance for human need. From the ecological perspective, the world as God's body is the concept embodying distributive justice while caring for the oppressed and the estranged.

The world as God's body in this environmental model is based on the internal relationship, not the external one. The internal relationship means that one's whole existence is constituted by and dependent on all others. They are not the meeting of a substance with other substances. Just as a stomach or liver is the internal constitutive organ of our body, my being is internally related with all the others.

This relationship derives form the God-world relationship as incarnational. McFague writes that "an interpretation of the God-world relationship based on the basic belief that God is incarnate in the world implies rethinking the issues of creation and providence in light of the world as internally related to God—the world as within God or the world as God's 'body'—rather than externally related as an artist is to his or her production."[12] Creation and providence manifest the God-world internal relationship in which God nourishes the world as God's body. God dynamically works in all the internal constituents of the elements comprising the world. This means that God and I, you and I, and the Earth and I are not two independent entities. They are internally related in the process of God's creation and providence. Jesus' message that "I am in my Father, and you in me, and I in you" (John 14: 20) implies such an internal relationship. God and the world are interrelated not as two different substances but as one organic unity.

Ecologically speaking, a paradoxical relationship is deeply associated with its internal and intrinsic relationship. McFague says,

> The model of creation as God's body radicalizes both God's transcendence and God's immanence. This model has been criticized by some as pantheistic, as identifying God and the world. I do not believe it is. If God is to the universe as each of us is to our bodies, then God and the world are not identical. They are, however, intimate, close, and internally related in ways that can make Christian uncomfortable when it forgets its incarnationalism. But we Christians should not shy away from a model that radically underscores both divine transcendence and divine immanence.[13]

It is paradoxical that God's transcendence is internally related to God's immanence. God's transcendence does not come into play outside the world. God's transcendence has its value and meaning within the dynamics of the world. God's transcendence and immanence are the dipolar characteristics of

God's interaction with the world. In other words, they are the two different divine modes embodied in the world. While God's transcendence compares to God's mind, God's immanence compares to God's body. Just as mind and body can never be separable in their conditions, so God's transcendence and immanence are both aspects of one reality working in and through the world.

God's transcendent aspect is embodied in the planet Earth where we live. According to McFague, "The most radically transcendent understanding of God is, then, at the same time the most radically immanent understanding."[14] The transcendent God can never be separated from our living space by incarnating and embodying God's self into the world we live in. God's eternal and perfect love and goodness is the example of God's transcendent aspect that may be distinguished from the imperfect situation of our world. Such a transcendent aspect, however, reveals its meaning and value in God's incarnational nature developed *in and through* the world. Hodgson says,

> Reality as a whole is a complex interplay of dimensions, which can neither be reduced to the one-dimensional picture of traditional science nor be divided into the two-dimensional worldview of traditional theology—the supernatural and the natural, the eternal and the temporal, the sacred and the profane. Instead dimensional analysis should be expanded to include psychological, cultural, ethical, aesthetic, and religious or spiritual aspects of reality, all of which interact in complex ways.[15]

God's aim to lead the world into God's goodness, which is God's transcendent nature, inspires God's incarnation down to Earth. The world as God's body is not static but transformative in response to God's plan. In this way, God's transcendence from and immanence in the world are organically interrelated. Thus, according to McFague, "because God is always incarnational, always embodied, we can see God's transcendence immanentally. Meeting God is not a momentary "spiritual" affair; rather God is the ether, the reality, the body, the garden in which we live."[16] The world in which we live is the body of God. The beauty of nature is embodied in the harmonious relation among all the organs of God's body. Air, mountains, rivers, trees, animals, persons are all the constituents of God's body. Their authentic relationship is made through mutual existence in support.

God's creation and providence, therefore, are based on God's organic relation to the world. As McFauge says,

> God is with us, here and now, in this world. Our doctrines of creation and providence do not stand alone: They are offshoots of our deepest beliefs about the nature of God's relation to the world. . . . If this belief is that God and the

world are intrinsically intimate, creation and providence will be understood from within that perspective.[17]

God's creation and providence can be understood by the analogy of a human body: all functions of each part or organ in the body should work together for the good of the whole body. People usually think that if they are sick from a stomachache, it originates in a problem with the stomach. However, the stomach is organically related to the other organs. All organs in our body cannot be separated but are deeply associated. Disease of the stomach, liver, or intestines is not only due to a problem with one part but also from the loss of harmony with all other parts. Like this organic system of the body, the world is the place in which all components are organically interrelated. God's creation and providence are made in the on-going process in which we preserve all natural resources as the constituents of God's body. God's creation and providence basically undertake the human and natural world, which is organically interwoven by the organs of God's body. In this situation God's creation and providence refers to the creative transformation of the world in the harmony and order of God's body organs. Given this, God's transcendence cannot be understood without God's immanence in the world in which we live. In this way, God's transcendence and immanence are paradoxically combined with our ecological concerns.

A DIALOGUE BETWEEN CHRISTIANITY AND OTHER WORLD RELIGIONS IN THE ORGANIC MODEL

Ludwig Wittgenstein's (1889-1951) theory of language game developed in his *Philosophical Investigations* (1953) is insightful for understanding interreligious dialogue. According to Wittgenstein, we practice the usage of words employed in linguistic activity such as questioning, naming, ordering and also in learning how words are employed in contexts. Learning language is playing the "language-game." Wittgenstein defines this language-game as "consisting of language and the actions in which it is woven, the language-game."[18] A word is like a chess piece, and "the meaning of a piece is its role in the game."[19] The language game refers to the phenomena of language used differently in different contexts. These phenomena do not have a common quality but at most a "family resemblance." Wittgenstein insists that the concepts of words do not denote sharply fixed substances but rather note family resemblances between the things named with the concepts. The use of language is established upon the language game and family resemblances.[20]

Wittgenstein asserts that if we drive the language given to ourselves into a formalized pattern on the basis of our conceptualizing and theorizing minds, we can fall into the fallacy of reducing a diversity of language uses to a one-sided, oversimplified view wherein we pursue the essentialism of language. In this sense, according to Wittgenstein, concepts are flexible or elastic. "For in the flux of life, where all our concepts are elastic, we couldn't reconcile ourselves to a rigid concept."[21] Because words are deeply rooted in a pattern of life, they contain the characteristic of indefiniteness, because the pattern of life is not always formed in regularity. Language is part of the dynamic process in conjunction with the forms of life.

This view of language maintains that we cannot solve all the philosophical problems from the sheer clarification of language just as we cannot cut off everything with a sharpened knife. For Wittgenstein, philosophy has overlooked the obscure aspect of language, thereby eliminating its ambiguity and driving it to lucidity in reductive ways apart from its given circumstances. The description of a word is the description of a certain system or circumstance. For instance, simplicity and complexity do not have the absolute quality of existing in the thing itself. We use the two words in a number of different ways according to various contexts in which one shows its meanings in relation to the other.[22]

This perspective of language is very important for theological discourse. All religious language referring to God is metaphorical. Its fixed meanings lose the rich contexts of language and further prevent a certain tradition from proceeding to a dynamically living tradition. Metaphors are used to convey what is unknown through the words known to us. They are contextual and may have different significances outside a certain context or tradition.

Theology in the organic model entails a paradigm shift from the mechanistic model in which God and the world are static. The symbols conveying the deep layer of the mind inspire the organic relationship between God and the world. They also play an important role in forming a shared community binding each individual. According to Edward Farley,

> Deep symbols do continue to empower the language of at least some communities and some movements of cultural criticism. Appeals to such symbols continue to be made in the public sphere, and these appeals are not without their power. Furthermore, it appears to be the case that the post modern has not abolished the matrix of deep symbols, the sphere of relation and the interhuman. In the sphere of the interhuman, human beings relate to each other, not merely as functionaries in a preprogrammed bureaucracy, but in mutual perceptions of their vulnerability, needs, pathos, possibilities, and mystery. In the sphere of relation human beings continue to experience mutual obligation, guilt and resentment, gratitude, limitations on their autonomy, and mutual activities of creativity. From such relations are born notions of personhood, justice, mutual obligation, and even truth and reality.[23]

Farley calls the people in symbolic relationship "the interhuman," which does not mean simply a meeting between different individuals but the organic relationship in which others constitute me and vice versa. From each moment (that we breathe) in to our mental activity, we are interwoven in every way imaginable through "the matrix of deep symbols." For Christianity, the cross plays a crucial role in forming a shared community from their worship services through bodily behaviors (i.e., singing, eating taking communion) to their moral behavior and spiritual experiences. For Buddhism, the image of Buddha is the great symbol to convey the meaning of emptiness that invites their meditation (practicing a peaceful moment in each step) and inspire their spiritual performance to free from human greed. For (Neo) Confucianism, both material force (*qi*) and principle (*li*, i.e., righteousness, inner integrity, love of humanity, altruism, and loyalty) form a shared community and value for East Asians.

This sphere of interhuman is also applied to the God-human relationship in the Christian tradition. Farley says,

> If personhood is defined in terms of intrinsic relations with others, then to think of God as personal in no sense implies a being separated from other beings who relates externally and distantly to them, in the way that the king-realm personal model suggests. On the contrary, it suggests, I believe, that God is present in and to the world as the kind of other, the kind of Thou, much closer to a mother, lover, or friend than to a king or lord. The intrinsic, interdependent relationships we know most about are also the most intimate, interpersonal ones: they are the ones that begin, support, and nurture life.[24]

Through a variety of metaphors and images, God has an intrinsic and personal relationship with the world. Personhood cannot be defined without "intrinsic relations with others," and God also relates a "Godself" to the world through His or Her personal images. God is understood through metaphors in "an attempt to say something about the unfamiliar in terms of the familiar, an attempt to speak about what we do not know in terms of what we do know."[25] "The assumption here is that all talk of God is indirect: no words or phrases refer directly to God, for God-language can refer only through the detour of a description that properly belongs elsewhere."[26] God as the infinite cannot be exhaustively expressed by our language. Our direct reference to God may miss some other aspects of God.

Therefore, our expression of the infinite makes room for various metaphors according to each different community and tradition.

> The language of reality in any specific community reflects that community's paradigm of reality. Natural science, Zen Buddhism, the American transcendentalists,

and liberation theology each is working with a quite different paradigm of reality.[27]

Thus, the truth is always open to a larger and broader interpretation by learning one another's contexts and traditions.

This claim about truth evokes comparative theology and interreligious dialogue. For the performance of comparative theology and interreligious dialogue, "emic" and "etic" points of view can help set a method to understand different traditions.[28] While emic points of view are exercised by an insider of a cultural and historical context, etic points of view are expressed by an outsider's approach to the cultural system.

Whereas emic rules of phonemes are formed by such phenomena as the difference between the English phonemes /p/ and /b/, etic rules of phonemes ascribe such differences to similar data in spoken English. According to Kenneth Pike, "Descriptions or analyses from the etic standpoint are alien, with criteria external to the system. Emic descriptions provide an internal view, with criteria chosen from within the system. They represent to us the view of one familiar with the system and who knows how to function within it himself."[29] An etic system may be set up by criteria whose relevance is external to the system being studied. The discovery or setting up of the emic system requires the inclusion of criteria relevant to the internal functioning of the system itself. Pike says,

> The etic organization of a worldwide cross-cultural scheme may be created by the analyst. The emic structure of a particular system must, I hold be discovered. . . . Descriptions or analyses from the etic standpoint are alien, with criteria external to the system. Emic descriptions provide an internal view, with criteria chosen from within the system. They represent to us the view of one familiar with the system and who knows how to function within it himself. . . . An etic system may be set up by criteria whose relevance is external to the system being studied. The discovery or setting up of the emic system requires the inclusion of criteria relevant to the internal functioning of the system itself. . . . The etic view does not require that every unit be viewed as part of a larger setting. The emic view, however, insists that every unit be seen as somehow distributed and functioning within a larger structural unit or setting.[30]

From this distinction between emic and etic, a method for the discipline of comparative theology is available in terms of different emical settings (for each different tradition). Of course, etic points of view provide advantages to finding similarities between two different religious traditions, such as Christianity and Buddhism. Yet, those similarities can also allow distorting specific (or original) meanings of the terms developed in the different religious traditions, by etically ascribing two different religious terms to similar or same data from the outsider's perspective. Two different religious traditions need to be examined by respecting the each other's differences at an equal level (from the insider's point of view).

In his approach to comparative theology, Robert Neville attempts to combine etic with emic views. Neville acknowledges not only that religious cultures differ but also that the circumstances of their historical contexts mean that they truly are different worlds, although perhaps today we are beginning to develop a shared world. Therefore there will be limitations on our ability to know the full range of another's religion. However, Neville wants to positively accept such limitations since they enable scholars to enter to some degree into various communities of faith without being reduced by them. Neville attempts to make explicit a new religious path in Western culture involving a combination of philosophical theology (etic) and the history of religions (emic).

Yet, the assumption that Neville often starts with in developing his comparative theology is "creation ex nihilo" as "the model of world, source, and creative act." According to Neville, creation ex nihilo means creative activity with "the world created, the source of creation, and the activity itself, which are indissolubly united."[31] He presents this motif of creation ex nihilo as a reconciling factor between theistic and non-theistic tradition. Neville strives to develop his own all-embracing interpretative framework within which he can approach and investigate other religious traditions.

Neville's proposed metaphysical base is driven by his etic points of view in which the Buddhist meaning "Emptiness is Form" developed in its own tradition may be reduced under the notion of "creation ex nihilo," although it enriches the Christian-Buddhist dialogue.

"Differences" from each emic point of view (an insider's view for each different tradition) need to be accentuated for studying two different religious traditions. Their uniqueness transforms their own tradition in the dialogue performed by admitting and respecting each other's identity and life. In this encounter, a religious tradition can learn about differences of the other religious experience and enrich one's own experience.

In the correlation of Christianity and non-Christian religions, Schineller classifies Christology into exclusive Christology, inclusive Christology, normative Christology and non-normative Christology. Exclusive Christology believes that the salvation paradigm of Christianity is the only way to salvation, and that the salvation paradigms of other religions are deceitful ways leading to failure. On the other hand, inclusive Christology shows that the new life and power of truth, which are revealed in the life, death, and the resurrection of Jesus Christ, cannot be confined within doctrinal systems or fundamentalist principles. "Jesus Christ is constitutive of the word of God in the world. He is the mediator of all other revelations, and salvation which can be attained in the world first occurs in Jesus and occurs elsewhere only through him."[32] Though this position is not exclusive of other religious contexts, it does not indicate the opening up of new horizons for mutual transformation but it insists on Christ as the unique savior above all other religious truths and values. According to Karl Rahner, "If one believes seriously in the universal salvific purpose of God toward all men in Christ, it need not and cannot really be doubted that gratuitous influences of properly Christian supernatural grace are conceivable in the life of all men."[33] For Rahner, Christian supernatural grace is thoroughly beyond all religious contexts. The salvific power of Christ cannot be relativized in light of non-Christian contexts. It is regarded as the universal and ultimate truth, which is both the starting and ending point of any interreligious dialogue , above various religious truths and values.

Furthermore, Rahner writes that "the world is drawn to its spiritual fulfillment by the Spirit of God, who directs the whole history of the world in all its length and breadth towards its proper goal."[34] That is to say, non-Christian religions are not complete, in order that they can be made clear and complete in Christ.

Non-Christian traditions, however, have their own culture and context for understanding and interpreting the Salvific figure. In other words, the interreligious dialogue with respect to traditional religions should focus on how to share and open up a new horizon of religious experience rather than interpret non-Christian contexts under Christ in the name of a universal salvific figure.

Schineller's third position—the Theocentric universe, normative Christology—emphasizes Jesus not as the "constitutive" but as the normative expression of God by correcting mediations of other religions by considering other truths and values of non-Christian contexts in light of the Theocentric perspective, not the Christocentric one. Schineller writes that

> Jesus is not constitutive of man's salvation but represents and reveals decisively ad normatively the universal love of God. The absence of the Christ event would not imply or result in the absence of grace, but rather the absence of the decisive manifestation of grace. . . . Salvation, which was always possible for all mankind, becomes decisively and normatively manifest in Jesus. . . . In so far as Christ is normative, the church can be considered the normative way of salvation.[35]

In other words, the Theocentric universe-normative Christology view does not accept the view that the traditional culture was dominated by demonic powers before its encounter with Christianity. Yet, the traditional culture and the present world are still defined as being less normative than Christ. They are the objects, which are transformed by the power of Jesus Christ. While Christ is the normative way to transforming the subject, the traditional culture is the object to be transformed.

For Schineller's fourth position, however, the Theocentric universe-non-normative Christology, he claims that "Judgments about claims to uniqueness or normativeness are unverifiable and without basis.... There are many mediators of salvation and Jesus Christ is one of them."[36] There are diverse ways for humankind to attain a religious experience of salvation and religious insights. God is understood through our finite situation, and we experience God in our context. Because God as a being itself is infinite, humans cannot exhaustively define the infinite God, for humanity itself is limited to context. Immanuel Kant says, "We cannot positively extend the sphere of the objects of our thought beyond the conditions of our sensibility, that is, noumena, since such objects have no assignable positive meaning."[37] Even our religious experience, as well as our thinking based on pure reason, cannot grasp God as the Eternal One in the noumenal world. John Hick writes,

> The Eternal One is the divine noumenon which is experienced and thought within the different religious traditions as the range of divine phenomena witnessed to by the religious history of mankind.... we have no fully tradition-neutral or tradition-transcending term. One is therefore obliged to use a term provided by a particular tradition, but to use it (consciously to misuse it) in a way which moved beyond the bounds of that tradition.... We shall in fact, I believe, be led to distinguish between God, and God as conceived and experienced by human beings. God is neither a person nor a thing, but is transcendent reality which is conceived and experienced by different human mentalities in both personal and nonpersonal ways.[38]

We understand God as the Ultimate from our historical and cultural backgrounds. Our experiences of God have a cultural ground with various features. While the ultimate reality is in the noumenal area beyond the horizons of our awareness, we experience the Ultimate as the One, which is deeply embedded in our traditions as the Many. "Traditional-neutrality" is beyond human capacity, for our religious experience is mediated by familial, communal, religious, and cultural traditions. In this context, the phenomena of religious experience varies according to human history and culture. According to Gadamer,

> In fact, we belong to history long before we understand ourselves in a self-evident way in the family, society, and state in which we live. The focus of subjectivity is a distorting mirror. The self-awareness of the individual is only a flickering in the closed circuits of historical life. That is why the prejudices of the individual constitute the historical and cultural reality of his being.[39]

We are influenced by our own culture and history, whether or not we are conscious of its impact. In our experience of God, we cannot avoid contextualizing God in terms of our culture and history. This signifies that we understand God separately from cultural and historical systems, and our experience of God must take into account such existential, cultural and historical situations of humanity. The Ultimate has many names.

> Jesus' religious significance would probably have been expressed by hailing him within Hingu culture as a divine avatar and within the Mahayana Buddhism which was then developing in India as a Bodhisattva, if the Christian gospel had moved into India. . . . The value of the incarnational doctrine is not indicative but expressive.[40]

Human beings' ultimate concerns appear differently in various religious traditions. Our understanding of God reflects the diversity of God's ways within the various streams of human life. Thus we should have an openness to the various types of salvation experiences revealed in the religious history of humankind. Our religious openness, moreover, should be based on our organic relationship and sharing with other religious experiences.

In this sense, Schineller's nonnormative Christology opens rather objective and fair interreligious dialogue by acknowledging human epistemological limitations. However, Schineller considers nonnormative Christology to be another extreme position against exclusivism, since epistemological relativism leads to skepticism on salvific figures revealed in each religious tradition, so that we cannot decide any normative way. Schineller points out that

> It is impossible or unnecessary to judge among religions and salvific figure. . . . It prefers let God be God; it cautions against making God and His Ways into our image, and against trying to judge Him and His ways into our image, and against trying to judge Him and His ways by our human standards. . . . The fourth position, where Jesus is one of many mediators, seems somewhat ineffective in an age of pluralism, since it affirms that we cannot make decisions among religions and religious savior figures.[41]

Schineller seems to assume that judgments or decisions are the preconditions of interreligious dialogue. Of course, nonnormative Christology can lead to relativism or skepticism, which also may weaken our commitment to our savior figure. In this context, the religious dimension is not confined to the objectivity or parity of interreligious dialogue. It is continuously being developed by our commitment to the uniqueness of the Ultimate, in which we put our faith.

However, the uniqueness of Jesus does not necessarily lead to normative Christology. Jesus' life is distinct from Confucius', Laozi's, Gautama

Siddhartha's, or Mohammad's. Their messages have their uniqueness, each truth claim of which refers to the whole of the ultimate reality. Thus, interreligious dialogue is neither the issue of which salvific figure is normative and superior, nor the problem of making judgments on the genuine salvific figure. Nonnormative Christology is not necessarily connected with relativism or skepticism. Nonnormative Christology conversely implies that there are many ways leading to the Ultimate, so that this position can be an opportunity to reform and develop our own religious tradition by learning other truths or norms. In other words, interreligious dialogue works rather in a dialectical way to enrich the religious experiences of both parties than in an attempt to answer the question of which salvific way is normative. We can learn other ways and develop our own traditions in the context of non-normative Christology in which various norms and values in different traditions can be fused together. The interreligous dialogue can be a dimension revealing the paradoxical and dialectical ways of various religious traditions.

The human religious context is never static or closed; it is always open to newer and deeper experiences of the Ultimate Reality. We are constituted in and through our traditions. However, each tradition has a dynamic relationship with other traditions. We have our own view of the past and present cultural traditions. We should continue to open our own views through the encounter with other views.

In this structure of tradition, our religious experiences are carried out by all medicacy and immediacy. The immediacy and meditation continuously and dynamically drives our religious experience. As David Tracy writes,

> if we are to know Jesus as he was and is, we must know him through the mediation of the whole tradition as witness to him and immediately as we have ourselves experienced him either individually or communally in our experience of the Christ event as from God and happening now.[42]

Tracy shows that our awareness of Jesus is formed by the past and the present mediated by the tradition. This, of course, does not mean that we are confined by our traditions, for tradition itself is not understood in a fixed frame but in a dynamic structure.

The whole tradition as mediacy and individual or communal experiences as immediacy constitute our religious experience in a dynamic relationship with others, in which we learn the religious experiences of others and expand our religious horizons. According to Tracy, "If the always-already, not-yet reality of grace decisively disclosed in the Christ event the focal meaning of Christian self-understanding, then that actuality must imply Christian theologians to enter into conversation with all the other religions and other classics."[43] The Christ event is not a finished or completed event. It unceasingly approaches

Christian self-understanding in the life situation. The always-already and not-yet reality of grace opens the way to all the truths in the ultimate reality. Here we can find the meaning of interreligious dialogue, for other religions also reflect and encompass the ultimate reality in their own context.

With regard to religious classics, Tracy maintains that "every religious classic recognizes itself not as its own but as a gift and command from and by the power of the hole."[44] In other words, each religious context shows only the fact and values limited to its context, but refers to "the power of the whole," which makes multi-dimensional religious experiences converge. Thus, according to Cantwell Smith,

> To understand Buddhists, we must look not at something called Buddhism but at the world; so far as possible, through Buddhist eyes. For this, we must among other matters learn to use the total system of Buddhist doctrine or world-view as Buddhists use it; as a pattern for ordering the data of observation.[45]

Since Buddhism does not say only for itself but for the whole world, we should be able to listen to and learn their truth through their eyes.

> To be a Christian means to participate in the Christian process, just as to be a Muslim means to participate in the Islamic process; to be a Jew, in the Jewish; and so on, and on. . . . To be Christian or Muslim or Buddhist, to be religious, is a creative act, of participation in a community in motion.[46]

A Christian constitutes his or her own identity in the process of becoming a Christian. That is, being and becoming are mutually interrelated in the process of creative transformation. "Learning in the humanities involves being open to that which may be greater than oneself; greater, at least, than one has been until now. The process of knowing is a process of becoming."[47] Knowing always expands its horizons in relation to other horizons and differences in the process of becoming.[48]

NOTES

1. Mary Evelyn Tucker and John Grim, "Series Forward," in *Buddhism and Ecology: The Interconnection of Dharma and Deeds* eds. Mary Evelyn Tucker and Duncan Ryuken Williams (Harvard University Press, 1997), xix.

2. Sallie McFague, *Life Abundant: Rethinking Theology and Economy for a Planet in Peril* (Minneapolis: Fortress Press, 2001), 146

3. Sallie McFague, *Super, Natural Christians: How we should love nature* (Minneapolis: Fortress Press, 1997), 107.

4. McFague, *Life Abundant*, 101.

5. Duncan Ryuken Williams, "Introduction," in *Buddhism and Ecology*, xxvii.

6. Peter C. Hodgson, *Christian Faith: A Brief Introduction* (Louisville, KY: Westminster John Knox Press, 2001), 53.

7. Sallie McFague, "Is God in Charge: Creation and Providence" in *Essentials of Christian Theology*, ed. William C. Placher (Louisville: Westminster John Knox Press, 2003), 110.

8. Ibid., 111.

9. Ibid.

10. Ibid., 112.

11. Sallie McFague, *The Body of God: An Ecological Theology* (Minneapolis: Fortress Press, 1993), 164.

12. McFague, "Is God in Charge?: Creation and Providence" in *Essentials of Christian Theology*, 102.

13. Ibid., 113.

14. Ibid.

15. Hodgson, Christian Faith, 51.

16. McFague, "Is God in Charge?: Creation and Providence" in *Essentials of Christian Theology*, 113.

17. Ibid., 102.

18. Ludwig Wittgenstein, *Philosophical Investigations*, trans. G. E. M. Anscombe (New York: Macmillan Publishing Co., Inc., 1968), 7.

19. Ibid., 563.

20. Ibid., 67.

21. Ibid., 246.

22. K. T. Fann, *Wittgenstein's Conception of Philosophy*, trans. Maurice Cranston (Notre Dame, Indiana: University of Notre Dame Press, 1986), 75-83.

23. Edward Farley, *Deep Symbols: Their Postmodern Effacement and Reclamation* (Valley Forge, Pennsylvania: Trinity Press International, 1996), 23.

24. Ibid., 84.

25. Ibid., 33-34.

26. Ibid.

27. Farley, Deep Symbols, 57.

28. Kenneth Pike first coined the term "emic" and "etic" in his book *Language in relation to a Unified Theory of the Structure of Human Behavior* (Glendale, CA: Summer Institute of Linguistics, 1954) and Marvin Harris employed and developed those terms in *Cultural Materialism* (New York: Random House, 1964).

29. Pike, *Language in relation to a Unified Theory of the Structure of Human Behavior*, 37.

30. Ibid.

31. Robert Neville, *Behind the Masks of God: An Essay toward Comparative Theology* (New York: State University of New York Press, 1991), 13.

32. Peter Schineller, "Christ and Church: A Spectrum of Views," in *Theological Studies* 37 (1976) 552.

33. Karl Rahner, "Christianity and Non-Christian Religions," in *Theological Investigations* 5 (New York: Seabury, 1974) 125..

34. Karl Rahner, "The One Christ and the Universality of Salvation," in *Theological Investigations*, 16 (New York: Seabury, 1979) 204.

35. Peter Schineller, "Christ and Church: A Spectrum of Views," in *Theological Studies* 37 (1976) 557-9.

36. Ibid., 560.

37. Immanuel Kant, *Critique of Pure Reason*, trans. Norman Kemp Smith (New York: St. Martin's Press, 1965), 292.

38. John Hick, *God Has Many Names* (Philadelphia: Westminster Press), 83, 91.

39. Hans Georg Gadamer, *Truth and Method*, trans. & eds. Garett Barden and John Cumming, (New York: The Crossroad Publishing Company, 1977), 245.

40. John Hick, "Jesus and the World Religions," in *Myth of God Incarnate*, eds. John Hick (Philadelphia: The Westminster Press, 1977), 176, 178.

41. Schineller, "Christ and Church: A Spectrum of Views," 560, 565.

42. David Tracy, *The Analogical Imagination: Christian Theology and the Culture of Pluralism* (New York: Crossroad, 1981), 236.

43. Ibid., 449.

44. Ibid., 249.

45. Wilfred Cantwell Smith, *Towards a World Theology: Faith and the Comparative History of Religion* (Maryknoll, NY: Orbis Books, 1981), 82.

46. Ibid., 34.

47. Ibid., 76.

48. We can notice the circular, symmetrical view of Buddhism from Buddhist Dharma-nature. "Since dharma-nature is round interpenetrating. It is without any sign of duality. No name and no form, All distinctions are abolished. In One is all, in Many is one." See Steve Odin, *Process Metaphysics and Hua-yen Buddhism* (Albany, NY: State University of New York Press, 1982), 9. This circular view of Buddhism is based on a different paradigm from the linear and asymmetrical view of Christianity. In this situation, more important issue for the dialogue of Buddhism and Christianity is to learn other paradigms and proceeds at the level of life-producing realities rather than to elucidate whether symmetrical or asymmetrical view is right at the level of doctrine.

Conclusion

Paradoxes or ambiguities are potential sources for the creative encounters between different religious traditions on a cross-cultural basis. A self means the relational self; it is constituted by interdependent relations with other cosmic events by way of which opposite elements are organically combined. This structure of self in the organic model is not confined in logical consistency. It is based on correlative thinking with a focus on concrete contexts formed in the empirical world. The relational self is the self constituting its character in difference, which is not regarded as exclusive but correlative with self-identity.

The beauty of balance is based on the organic relation in the concrete world where the self dynamically moves with the correlation of the opposites. Therefore, balance is not an abstract concept but is a contextual notion rooted in our life world. The source for the beauty of balance is in the interchangeability of opposite things. The opposite is not the substantial opposite but the relational opposite that can be interchangeable with its different aspects in dynamic tension, thereby contextually defined in the correlative manner.

All factors in the universe operate with their value system in balance and harmony with one another. The formation of a pattern in the empirical world and its endurance and transformation are required for the value-realization of things. A good pattern in balance includes the element that promotes the harmony and intensity of things by connecting all living worlds. In this sense, value loses its meaning without any relation and reference to a particular context. With the pattern of connecting the particular facts shown in each context, value lies in the transformative process of things that modify their contexts.

The beauty of balance is not clearly defined by the law of contrast. It is based on the "aesthetic complex" transforming logical inconsistency into creative moments. Such a transformation is achieved by appropriating logically inconsistent terms into the aesthetic context in which a self or one's own religious-cultural tradition enjoys the experience of novelty. Even if two different traditions are logically inconsistent, they can be transformed to the creative relation by their aesthetic enjoyment.

This view does not refer to an abstract value system but to the correlative system of the real concrete world. Harmony is not attained by a logical reductionism but in incorporating logical incongruities through the process of change. In this sense, paradox entails the transformation of one's own religious tradition by encountering a different world that cannot be easily described in logical consistency and scientific rationality. The ambiguity of a religious concept in the encounter between different traditions is open to balance and transformation toward aesthetic harmony attuning different entities and opposite terms . This character of balance starts with an emphasis on particular contexts. It proceeds to a different path from development with the first principle with the assumption of universality.

To explore the beauty of balance, I discussed Hegel's dialectics and indicated its contributions and limitations to the encounter between different religious traditions. I presented Whitehead's philosophy of organism to supplement the problem of Hegel's Absolute Spirit. Whitehead's process thoughts in the organic model are carefully compared to Jung's depth psychology for the subject of divine paradox and harmony.

To analyze the issue of paradox in the relational paradigm, I explained Bateson's theory of double binding and examined why a paradoxical situation occurs and how it can be solved in his idea of metapattern. Bateson's metapattern or metacontext enhances the organic relation between the opposites, which triggers the encounter of the West with the East. In particular, discussing Ilbu Kim's "Jeongyeokdo" and Wonhyo's "Huajaeing" theory in relation to Korean religious thoughts, I demonstrated that paradox is not a subject to be eliminated but a potential and creative source for the beauty of balance between the opposites.

Finally, I presented the theological significance of dialogue in the organic model. I discussed two types of dialogue: the dialogue between Christianity and nature, and the dialogue between Christianity and other world religions. Environmental ethics and interreligious dialogues are two contemporary issues that we are faced with. Among those dialogues are included a number of contrasting characters and elements in their differences. Yet, the purpose of dialogues between differences is not the simple addition of opposites but their creative transformation. Above all, the dialogues should be contextually rooted in the concrete world. They are not based on the mechanistic model but on the organic model in which all different elements produce a transformed and new life. This organic model performs to learn and respect the others for enriching one's own tradition; it retrieves all the fringes overlooked by traditional Christianity based on fundamentalist conservatism and anti-cultural triumphalism. Simply focusing on the absolute sovereignty of God and the Scripture do not help to answer religious conflicts or our contemporary practical issues, such as the ecological crisis.

To know Christianity, we need to know the organic relation between human beings and nature as God's creatures. To know Christianity, we need to know the organic relation between Christianity and other religio-cultural contexts. One's own identity is formed by its relation to others. Identifying the nature of Jesus' words is meaningless without knowing its contextual relation. Likewise, the significance of Jesus' message comes from his words rooted in our world. For this reason, it is important for us to raise the question of where we are (the circumstances with which we are currently faced) and how we are related to other religious contexts and nature, interpreting and applying divine reality to diverse contexts.

The opposite elements perform another pattern of order in their organic relation, which embodies the sense of order in its particular details. These particular details convey a diversity of contexts: religious contexts, natural surroundings, and socio-cultural environments. The pattern or order formed in particularity exhibits the relation between the divine and diverse contexts in their paradoxical situations and reveals the beauty of their balance and transformation.

Selected Bibliography

Ames, Roger T. "The Classical Chinese Self and Hypocrisy," in *Self and Deception: a cross-cultural philosophical enquiry*, ed. Roger T. Ames and Wilmal Dissanayake. Albany, NY: SUNY, 1996.

An English Translation of Fa-Tsang's Commentary on the Awakening of Faith, trans. Dirck Vorenkamp. Lewiston, New York, 2004.

Archetypal Process: Self and Divine in Whitehead, Jung, and Hillman, ed., David Ray Griffin. Evanston, Illinois: Northwestern University Press, 1989.

Bateson, Gregory. *Mind and Nature*. New York: E.D. Dutton.

———. *Steps to An Ecology of Mind*. New York: Chandler Publishing Company, 1972.

Bracken, Joseph A. *Christianity and Process Thought: Spirituality for a Changing World*. Philadelphia: Templeton Foundation Press, 2006.

Berthrong, John. *Concerning Creativity: A Comparison of Chu Hsi, Whitehead, and Neville*. Albany, NY: SUNY, 1998.

Buddhism and Ecology: The Interconnection of Dharma and Deeds eds. Mary Evelyn Tucker and Duncan Ryuken Williams. Harvard University Press, 1997.

Buswell, Robert. *The Formation of Ch'an Ideology in China and Korea*. Princeton, NJ: Princeton University Press, 1989.

Canon of Chun-Do-Kyo. Seoul: Chun-Do-Kyo General Assembly, 1970.

Casti, John L. *Complexification: Explaining a Paradoxical World through the Science of Surprise*. New York: HarperPerennial, 1995.

Chen, Yu-hui Chen. *Abolutes Nichts und rhythmisches Sein*. Berlin: Bamberg University, 1999.

Choi, Dong Hee, *History of Korean Religious Thought*, vol. 3, Chun-Do-Kyo. Seoul: Munwhasa, 1978.

Cobb, John and Griffin, David. *Process Theology: An Introductory Exposition* Philadelphia: The Westminster Press, 1976.

Duncan Ryuken Williams, "Introduction," in *Buddhism and Ecology*, ed. Mary Evelyn Tucker and Duncan Ryuken Williams. Cambridge, MA: Harvard University Press, 1998.

Farley, Edward. *Deep Symbols: Their Postmodern Effacement and Reclamation* (Valley Forge, Pennsylvania: Trinity Press International, 1996.

Gadamer, Hans Georg. *Truth and Method*, trans. & eds. Garett Barden and John Cumming. New York: The Crossroad Publishing Company, 1977.

Griffin, David R. "Buddhist Thought and Whitehead's Philosophy," *International Philosophical Quarterly*, 262-84. Vol. 14 (1974).

——. *God& Religion in the Postmodern World: Essays in Postmodern Theology*. Albany, NY: SUNY, 1989.

Gupta, Anil. "Truth and Paradox," in *Recent Essays on Truth and the Liar Paradox*, ed. Robert L. Martin, 175-237. New York: Clarendon Press, 1984. .

Hall, David L. and Ames, Roger T. *Thinking Through Confucius* (Albany, NY: SUNY, 1987.

Knox, T.M. "Translator's Preface," in Hegel, *Aesthetics: Lecture on Fine Art*, trans. T. M. Knox, vol. 1. Oxford: Clarendon Press, 1999.

Farley, Edward. *Deep Symbols: Their Postmodern Effacement and Reclamation*. Valley Forge, Pennsylvania: Trinity Press International, 1996.

Fan, K. T. *Wittgenstein's Conception of Philosophy*, trans. Maurice Cranston. Notre Dame, Indiana: University of Notre Dame Press, 1986.

Hall, "On the Academics of Deception," in *Self and Deception: a cross-cultural philosophical enquiry*, ed. Roger T. Ames and Wilmal Dissanayake. Albany, NY: SUYNY, 1996.

Harris, Marvin. *Cultural Materialism*. New York: Random House, 1964.

Hegel G. W. F. *Lectures on the Philosophy of Religion, One-Volume Edition The Lectures of 1827*, ed. Peter C. Hodgson. Berkeley, CA: University of California Press, 1988.

——. *Phenomenology of Spirit*, trans. A. V. Miller. Oxford: Oxford University Press, 1977.

——. *The Encyclopaedia Logic: Part I of the Encyclopaedia of Philosophical Sciences with Zusatze*, trans. T.F. Geraets, W.A. Suchting, & H.S. Harris. Cambridge: Hackett Publishing Company, Inc.

Hertzberger, Hans G. Hertzberger. "Truth and Modality in Semantically Closed Languages," in *The Paradox of the Liar*, ed. Robert L. Martin. 24-45. New Haven, NJ: Yale University Press, 1970.

Hick, John. *God Has Many Names*. Philadelphia: Westminster Press.

——. "Jesus and the World Religions," in *Myth of God Incarnate*, eds. John Hick Philadelphia: The Westminster Press, 1977.

Hodgson, Peter C. *Christian Faith: A Brief Introduction* (Louisville, KY: Westminster John Knox Press, 2001), 53.

——. "Georg Wilhelm Friedrich Hegel" in *Nineteenth Century Religious Thought in the West*, ed. Ninian Smart, vol. 1, 82-93. Cambridge: Cambridge University Press, 1985.

———. *G. W. F. Hegel Theologian of the Spirit*. Minneapolis: Fortress Press, 1997. 8-10.

———. "Logic, History, and Alternative Paradigms in Hegel's Interpretation of the Religions," 11-13. *AAR Nineteenth Century Theology Group 1992*.

———. *Winds of the Spirit: A Constructive Christian theology*. Louisville, Kentucky: Westminster John Knox Press, 1994.

Hosinski, Thomas E. *Stubborn Fact and Creative Advance: An Introduction to the Metaphysics of Alfred North Whitehead*. Lanham, Maryland: Rowman & Littlefield Publishers, Inc. 1993.

Houlgate, Stephen. *Freedom, Truth and History: An Introduction to Hegel's Philosophy* London: Routledge, 1991.

Ichijo, Ogawa. *Hodokesho Siso* (The Nature of Buddha). Tokyo: Humieido Publication, 1976.

Jaeschke, Walter. "Between Myth and History: On Hegel's Study of The History of Religion," 65-70. *AAR Nineteenth Century Theology Group 1992*.

Jung, Carl Gustav. *Memories, Dreams, and Reflections*, ed. Aniela Jaffe, trans. Richard and Clara Winstor. New York: Random House-Vintage Books, 1989.

Jung, Carl Gustav. *The Collected Works of C.G. Jung*, trans. R.F.C. Hullmet, 2d ed., Bollingens Series, vol. 11, *Answer to Job*. Princeton, NJ: Princeton University Press, 1969.

Kant, Immanuel. *Critique of Pure Reason*, trans. Norman Kemp Smith. New York: St. Martin's Press, 1965.

Kierkegaard, "Concluding Unscientific Postscript to the 'Philosophical Fragments'" in *A Kierkegaard Anthology*, ed. Robert Brentall. Princeton: Princeton University Press, 1973.

Kim, Sang Yil. *Chaos and Civilization: The Crisis of Civilization and the Resurrection of Chaotic Goddesses*. Seoul: Donga Publication, 1994.

———. *Cho Gong-gan gua Hangook Munwha* [*Trans-Space and Korean Culture*]. Seoul: Gyohak Yungusa, 1999.

———. *Dong-hak gua Shin-Seo-hak* [The Eastern and New Western Study] Seoul: Jishiksanupsa, 2000.

———. *I-Ching and the Logic of Postmodernism*. Seoul: Jishik Saneopsa, 2006.

———. *Russell Yok-sol gua Guahak Hyuk-myung ui Gujo* [Russell's Paradox and the Structure of Scientific Revolution]. Seoul: Sol Publications, 1997.

Kim, Young Choon. "An Analysis of Early Chun-Do-Kyo thought" in *Korea Journal* 17, no 10, 98-102. Seoul: Koryo, 1977.

Ko, Youngseop. "Wonhyo's Study of Unification," in *Wonhyo*. Seoul: Yemoon Seowon, 1993.

Leclerc, Ivor. *Whitehead's metaphysics: An Introductory Exposition* (London: George Allen and Unwin Ltd., 1958).

McFague, Salie. "Is God in Charge: Creation and Providence" in *Essentials of Christian Theology*, ed. William C. Placher, 110-120. Louisville: Westminster John Knox Press, 2003.

———. *Life Abundant: Rethinking Theology and Economy for a Planet in Peril* Minneapolis: Fortress Press, 2001.

———. *Super, Natural Christians: How we should love nature.* Minneapolis: Fortress Press, 1997.
———. *The Body of God: An Ecological Theology* (Minneapolis: Fortress Press, 1993), 164.
Neville, Robert. *Behind the Masks of God: An Essay toward Comparative Theology.* New York: State University of New York Press, 1991.
———. *Creativity and God: A Challenge to Process Theology.* Albany, NY: SUNY, 1995.
Odin, Steve. *Process Metaphysics and Hua-yen Buddhism.* Albany, NY: SUNY, 1982. Peter Schineller, "Christ and Church: A Spectrum of Views," in *Theological Studies* 37, 557-9 (1976).
Pike, Kenneth. *Language in relation to a Unified Theory of the Structure of Human Behavior.* Glendale, CA: Summer Institute of Linguistics, 1954.
Park, Sung Bae. *Buddhist Faith and Sudden Enlightenment.* Albany, NY: State University of New York, 1983.
———. *Wonhyo's Commentaries on the Awakening of Faith in Mahayana.* Ph.D. diss., University of California, 1979.
Philipson, Morris. *Outline of Jungian Aesthetics.* Evanston, IL: Northwestern University Press, 1963.
Rahner Karl. "Christianity and Non-Christian Religions," in *Theological Investigations* 5. New York: Seabury, 1974.
———. "The One Christ and the Universality of Salvation," in *Theological Investigations*, 16, 204-9. New York: Seabury, 1979.
Reynolds, Frank. Hegel Revisited: "A History of Religions/ Buddhist Studies Perspective," 108-110. *AAR Nineteenth Century Theology Group 1992.*
Russell, Bertrand. *Introduction to Mathematical Philosophy.* London: George Allen and Unwin LTD, 1960.
Schineller, Peter. "Christ and Church: A Spectrum of Views," in *Theological Studies* 37. 552-9, (1976).
Sherburne, Donald. *A Whiteheadian Aesthetic.* New Haven, NY: Yale University Press, 1961.
Simmons, Keith. *Universality and the Liar: An essay on truth and diagonal argument* New York: Cambridge University Press, 1993.
Smith, Wilfred Cantwell. *Towards a World Theology: Faith and the Comparative History of Religion.* Maryknoll, NY: Orbis Books, 1981.
Suchocki, Majorie Hewitt, *God Christ Church: A Practical Guide to Process Theology.* New York: Crossroad, 1989.
Takakusu, Junjiro. *The Essentials of Buddhist Philosophy*, ed. W.T. Chan and Charles A. Moore. Honolulu: University of Hawaii, 1947.
The Awakening of Faith. Trans. Yoshito S. Hakeda. New York: Columbia University Press, 1967.
The Classic of Changes : A New Translation of the I Ching As Interpreted by Wang Bi, trans. Richard John Lynn. New York: Columbia University Press, 1994.
Tracy, David. *The Analogical Imagination: Christian Theology and the Culture of Pluralism.* New York: Crossroad, 1981.

Whalen Wai-lun Lai, *The Awakening of Faith in Mahayana (T-ch'eng ch'i-hsin lun): A Study of the Unfolding of Sinitic Mahayana Motifs*. Ph.D. diss., Harvard University, 1975.
Whitehead, Alfred North. *Adventures of Ideas*. New York: The Free Press, 1993.
——. *Modes of Thoguht*. New York: The Free Press, 1968.
——. *Process and Reality*, ed. David Ray Griffin & Donald W. Sherburne. New York: The Free Press, 1978.
——. *Religion in the Making*. New York: Fordham University Press, 1996.
——. *Science and the Modern World*. New York: The Free Press, 1967.
——. *Symbolism: Its Meaning and Effect*. New York: Fordham University Press, 1985.
Whitehead, Alfred North Whitehead and Russell, Bertrand. *Principia Mathematica*, vol. 2. Cambridge, England: 1912.
Wilhelm Hellmut and Wilhelm Richard. *Understanding the I Ching [Yijing]: The Wilhelm Lectures of the Book of Changes*. Princeton, NJ: Princeton University Press, 1995.
Williamson, Raymond Keith. *Introduction to Hegel's Philosophy of Religion* (Albany, NY: SUNY, 1984.
Wittgenstein, Ludwig. *Philosophical Investigations*, trans. G. E. M. Anscombe. New York: Macmillan Publishing Co., Inc., 1968.
Wonhyo, "Expository Notes on the Awakening of Faith." In *The Collected Works of Korean Buddhism*, vol. 1, 747-760. Seoul: Dongguk University Publication, 2002.

Index

actual entities, 24, 26
actual occasions, 24
aesthetic complex, 61, 103
alaya-consciousness, 72–73
ambiguous self, 62
Ames, Roger, 59
archetypal form, 36
archetypal representation, 40
Aristotle's Law of Contrast, 1, 8, 17, 30, 55
Asanga, 77

Bateson, Gregory, 3, 44–53, 104
Becoming, 26, 29
Berthrong, John, 34
Bracken Joseph, 2, 22–24, 28–29
Buddha-mind, 72
Buddhism, 13, 16, 17, 18, 19, 29, 75, 77, 93, 98, 100
BUDDHIST-CHRISTIAN DIALOGUE, 10–19
Buswell, Robert, 74–75

Cartesian dualism, 83
causal efficacy, 32, 40–41
chaos, 23, 37
Che Chun-ju, 66–68
Choi, Jaewoo, 3, 66–69
Choi, Shi-young, 67

creation ex nihilo, 95
Christianity, 15, 57, 95–96, 98, 99, 104
Christology, 95–99
Chun-Do-Gyo, 66–68
Cobb, John, 33
Collective unconsciousness, 35, 38–39
Concrescence, 25, 26, 27, 39
Confucius, 54, 98
consummate religion, 15
contrasts of contrasts, 27
cosmos, 23
correlative cosmology, 83
correlative thinking, 60
creativity, 2, 22–29, 33–34

Dao, 58
Dharma, 75
Darwin, 68
depth psychology, 37
determinateness, 11
dipolar nature of God, 35
disorder, 23
divine quaternity, 30
Donghak, 3, 66–69

ecological, 83–90
ecosystem, 83
efficient causation, 25
ego-consciousness, 27, 30, 42

113

emic, 94–95
empiricism, 50
emptiness, 58
enlightenment, 73, 75
epistemological relativism, 98
essentialism, 92
eternal objects, 24
etic, 94–95
exclusivism, 98

family resemblance, 91
Farley, Edward, 92–93
final realities, 32
fullness, 58
Fu Xi, 54, 64

God's transcendence and immanence, 89–91
Good and evil, 22–24, 30, 34–36, 37
Griffin, David, 33, 39

Hakeda, Yoshito, 71
Hall, David, 51, 59, 61
Harmony, 103–4
Hegel, Georg Wilhelm Friedrich, 2, 6–21, 103
Hick, John, 97
Hodgson, Peter, 13, 15, 86
Hosinski, Thomas E., 25
Huayen, 18
Hume, David, 50
Hwajaeng, 4, 71, 75–80

Idealism, 7, 50
Ilbu Kim, 64–66, 104
individuation, 37, 39, 41
interhuman, 92–93
interpersonal, 93
interreligious dialogue, 4, 98–100, 103–4
intertheoretical vagueness, 51–52
Islam, 11

Jaeschke, Walter, 15
Jeongyeokdo, 3, 64–66, 103–4
Jesus, 83, 97–99, 104–5

Judaism, 11
Jung, Carl Gustav, 3, 35–41

Kierkegaard, Soren, 18
Kant, Immanuel, 56, 97
Kim, Ilbu, 3, 64–66, 103
Kim, Sang Yil, 55–58, 64–65

Laozi, 98
Li (Principle), 58, 93
Locke, John, 50
logical consistency, 60
logical reasoning, 7
logical Type, 44, 56

Madhyamika, 77
Mahayana, 77–79
McFague, Salie, 4, 83–90
metacontext, 44–45, 47, 48, 51–52
meta-language, 56
Mohammad, 99

Nagarjuna, 77
naturalism, 7
negation, 12
Neo-Confucianism. 58, 93
Neville, Robert, 30, 33, 34, 95
Newtonian-Cartesian scientific paradigm, 68
nirvana, 11–12
nonsensory perception, 39, 41
non-Euclidean, 65
normativeness, 97
noumena, 56
novelty, 23, 33

Odin, Steve, 35
order, 23, 37
organism, 50
ontological creativity, 33

pan-en-theism, 14, 16,
pantheism, 12, 16
paradox, 1, 4, 5, 24, 37, 52, 56, 57, 58, 80, 89, 103–4

Philosophical Investigations, 91
Pike, Kenneth, 94
Plato, 1, 62
prehension, 32, 33,
presentational immediacy, 33, 40–41
primordial nature, 27
Principia Mathematica, 44, 56
pure potentiality, 27

Qi (Material Force), 58, 93

reconciliation, 14
Rahner, Karl, 96
rationality, 8
reformed subjectivist principle, 26
relational self, 60
relativism, 98
Reynolds, Frank, 16
Russell, Bertrand, 3, 45

samsara, 11, 74, 80
satisfaction, 33
schimogenesis, 49
Schineller, Peter, 96–98
schizophrenic, 45, 46
scientific rationality, 61
self-reference, 56
self-annihilation, 56
self-denial, 88
self-emptiness, 88
sense-perception, 39, 40–41, 50, 62
Shih Chun-ju, 66–68
Siddhartha, Gautama, 99
Smith, Cantwell, 100
spirit, 6, 7, 9, 13, 24, 25
symbolic reference, 40
synchronicity, 40
synthesis, 2, 10, 13, 17

Tathagata (the Storehouse), 79
the Absolute Spirit, 2, 24, 25
the *Awakening of Faith*, 72–73
the Buddha nature, 75
the Concept, 7, 8, 9
the consequent nature, 14, 27, 33
the macrocosmic process, 25
the One Mind, 71–73, 75–76, 78–80
the organic model, 2, 87, 103–4
the mechanistic model, 104
the primordial nature, 14, 27, 33
the Euclidean method, 27
the Supreme Ultimate, 58, 64
the Universal Community, 24, 28
theocentric, 96–97
thusness, 78–80
T'iendai, 18
Tracy, David, 99
transition, 25, 26
trinity, 38
Troeltsch, Ernst, 18

unconsciousness, 30, 38

Vajrasamadhi-Sutra, 73, 75
value, 49–50, 63
Vasubandhu, 77
viscera, 41

Wilhelm, Hellmut, 54
Whitehead, Alfred, 2, 22–34, 37–43, 103
Wittgenstein, Ludwig, 91–92
Wonhyo, 71–82

Yang Chun-ju, 66–68
Yogacara, 77
Yijing (the Book of Changes), 3, 54–69
Yin and yang, 58–60, 64, 68–69